MICHAEL FARADAY

A LIST OF HIS LECTURES
AND PUBLISHED WRITINGS

━━◆╂ ╂◆━━

ALAN E. JEFFREYS

B.A., A.L.A.
Birmingham University Library

WITH A FOREWORD BY
SIR LAWRENCE BRAGG

O.B.E., M.C., D.Sc., F.R.S.

FIRST PUBLISHED 1960

Catalogue No. 657/4

Printed and bound in Great Britain by Jarrold & Sons Ltd, Norwich

MICHAEL FARADAY ESQ.
Painted and presented by
H.W. PICKERSGILL, R.A.
1830

FARADAY IN 1830 AT THE AGE OF 39
(from the portrait by H. W. Pickersgill at the Royal Institution)

for

S. M. J. *and* B. M. E. J.

FOREWORD

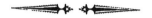

IN THIS BIBLIOGRAPHY of Michael Faraday's lectures and published writings, Mr. Jeffreys lists in chronological order his books, articles, papers, letters to the Press, lectures, and manuscript lecture notes. Though many biographies of Faraday have been written, such a list has never before been available to scholars, who have had to hunt for the material in numerous places. It starts in the year 1816, four years after Faraday came to the Royal Institution as Humphry Davy's assistant, and the last entry is for 1866, the year before his death. Mr. Jeffreys has added a list of the reprints or publications of his writings which appeared after his death, and a list of the main biographies.

The bare record of Faraday's writings year by year is in itself fascinating. It shows the breadth of his interest in a vast number of scientific subjects, and the many public services he performed as a scientific expert. The great years in which he was at the height of his powers stand out clearly. The index enables the student to find the references to his contributions on any particular subject. The value of such a work lies in the completeness of the record and of its index, and all who are interested in Faraday's life will be grateful to Mr. Jeffreys for the thoroughness and care with which he has made this excellent survey.

The Royal Institution   W. L. BRAGG
5th April, 1960

CONTENTS

LIST OF PLATES

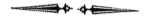

AUTHOR'S INTRODUCTION

SCOPE OF BIBLIOGRAPHY

THIS BIBLIOGRAPHY aims at recording in a single sequence and in strict chronological order (i) all books and separate publications, including later editions and reprints; (ii) all articles, papers, etc., in journals and periodical publications, including letters to such publications and to *The Times*; (iii) all lectures, whether they subsequently appeared in print or not; (iv) all the manuscript lecture notes in the Faraday Collection at the Royal Institution.

The bibliography is restricted to material published in English in Great Britain. Translations are not included, nor are American publications when the same work is published in Great Britain. Most of the personal letters of the kind such as are reprinted in Bence-Jones, *Life and letters of Faraday*, 1870, are excluded.

In listing later editions and reprints of material published as books I have avoided the intricacies of nineteenth-century publishing. I have approached nearest to such intricacies in listing the reprints of nos. 457 and 464 published by Chatto and Windus. This firm had both these items in print until 1925. It would seem that copies were bound up (often with a dated publisher's catalogue at the end) and issued as required, and that new sheets were printed when the stock of old ones was exhausted. A careful examination of a large number of copies of these two works might reveal small differences which would differentiate various reprints and issues.

Faraday does not seem to have been popular with bibliographers. The only bibliography which is at all comprehensive is by A. M. Lukomskaya and appears as an appendix to v. 2 of the Russian translation of *Experimental researches in electricity*, published by the Academy of Sciences of the U.S.S.R. in 1951.* The substance of this bibliography is in English and a knowledge of Russian is not necessary for its effective use.

Lukomskaya lists some 230 publications by Faraday and has about 170 references to biographical material. Material in languages other than English is included. In the list of works published by Faraday references to abstracts and reports are included as well as references to the original. This has sometimes resulted in the original and its abstract being listed as separate items (e.g. 67 and 69, 216 and 217). This is a sin to which the Royal Society's Catalogue of scientific papers is also prone. There is an occasional confusion in references to different items of like titles, e.g. 47 and 50, 206 and 214. 88 is the same as 90

---

* Экспериментальные исследования по электричеству, том 2, pp. 437-521. Библиографический указатель печатных трчдов Михаила Фарадея и основной литератчры о его жизни и деятельности.

and 147 is a part of 146. Apart from such minor blemishes, this bibliography, based entirely on the resources of Soviet libraries, is a noteworthy achievement.

Other works which may be mentioned are:

(1) *Royal Society's catalogue of scientific papers, 1800–1900.* This excludes books. It includes some published lectures but misses others, and sometimes duplicates entries by listing as different items the original and a translation or abstract (e.g. vol. 2, nos. 48 and 51, original and abstract).

(2) J. C. Poggendorff. *Biographisch-literarisches Handwörterbuch zur Geschichte der exacten Wissenschaften.* 1863–.

(3) P. F. Mottelay. *Bibliographical history of electricity and magnetism.* 1922.

Both of these have references to critical and biographical material as well as lists of Faraday's published books and articles. Poggendorff is the more useful. Mottelay's work is a narrative account with very many bibliographical references, but it suffers from the lack of a more disciplined order, and its references are too often brief to the point of obscurity.

(4) Finally there is a short bibliography published by the Pratt Institute, Brooklyn, *Michael Faraday, 1791–1867.* 1931.

The list of Faraday's lectures and published work following this Introduction was started at the Royal Institution in July 1956. It was continued and completed in Birmingham. It is based on the entries in the Royal Society's *Catalogue of scientific papers* together with the entries in the catalogues of the following libraries; the British Museum, the Royal Institution, the Institution of Electrical Engineers, the Universities of London and Birmingham, the Reference libraries of Southwark and Birmingham Public Libraries, and the Guildhall, London. I have also made use of the Pratt bibliography, Poggendorff and Mottelay, the bibliographies in *Isis; an international review devoted to the history of science,* and in the *Transactions of the Newcomen Society,* and the references in *Chemical Abstracts.* In addition I have consulted such published catalogues of the libraries of learned and scientific societies, etc., as I have come across.

Henry Bence-Jones in his *Life and letters of Faraday,* 2nd ed., 1870, gives for each year the number and often the titles of papers and lectures by Faraday. Unfortunately he omits all bibliographical information other than the title of the periodical in which a paper appeared. Since these "annual returns" by Bence-Jones are more comprehensive than any of the bibliographical aids mentioned above, the final stage in the compilation of the bibliography was a check through a number of scientific and other periodicals. The most important of these is the *Quarterly journal of science* which was edited and published from the Royal Institution. Faraday contributed many short anonymous articles to this journal which are not included in the Royal Society's *Catalogue of scientific papers.* I also hope to have rescued some published lectures from oblivion (e.g. nos. 336 and 351).

With the exception of nos. 209, 405, and 461, and some editions of nos. 297, 457, and 464, I have inspected all the items listed in the bibliography.

FARADAY'S PUBLISHED WORK

Books

Amid the mass of Faraday's published output there is only one book (*Chemical manipulation*, no. 153) in the sense of a monograph work appearing as such on its first publication. The majority of the items in this bibliography are for periodical articles, for papers read at meetings of societies, and for lectures. Faraday published in book form two collections of periodical articles and papers (*Experimental researches in electricity*, no. 297; and, *Experimental researches in chemistry and physics*, no. 458). Items which were reprinted in these collections are so noted in the bibliography. Some lectures also subsequently appeared in book form (e.g. *Chemical history of a candle*, no. 464).

Articles in periodicals

These are of two kinds: those to which Faraday appended his name or initials and those to which he did not. Where an article is signed by the initials "M.F.", with no other indication of authorship, I have indicated the item, "signed M.F.".

There is no reason to doubt the ascription to Faraday of articles signed M.F. We have his own word that this was his practice with articles which he did not consider to be of great importance. In the *Quarterly journal of science* for 1827, new series, vol. 2, p. 469, he refers to a previous article and says; "I did not esteem it of such importance as to put more than my initials to this account." Some of the articles reprinted in *Experimental researches in electricity* originally appeared with only the initials M.F. appended, e.g. Electromagnetic current, *Quart. j. sci.* 1825, vol. 19, p. 338 (no. 120). Similarly in the *Experimental researches in chemistry and physics* the article Boracic acid, *Quart. j. sci.* 1819, vol. 6, p. 152 (no. 39). Finally there is an editorial note on Faraday's behalf in the *Philosophical Magazine*, 1832, vol. 11, p. 236, which indicates that Faraday sometimes signed his articles with his initials (see below, p. xvi).

Where neither Faraday's name nor his initials are attached to an article I have noted the item "unsigned" and have given the reason for assigning it to Faraday. All these anonymous articles are from the *Quarterly journal of science*.

Faraday's authorship may be demonstrated in two ways: (1) By evidence from the cumulative index to vols. 1–20, 1816–26 of the *Quarterly journal of science*. (2) By evidence from a collection of periodical articles by Faraday in the Faraday Collection at the Royal Institution. There is also a copy of *Experimental researches in chemistry and physics* with annotations by Faraday in the library of the Institution of Electrical Engineers. These annotations occasionally (e.g. nos. 22, 259 and 154) reveal Faraday's authorship of an anonymous article.

(1) The *Quarterly journal of science* was edited and published from the Royal Institution. It started in 1816 with the title *Journal of science and the arts* and became the *Quarterly journal* ... in 1819 with vol. 7.

A cumulative index to vols. 1–20, 1816–26, was published in 1826. The copy of this index at the Royal Institution has added in manuscript on its title-page "Made by M. Faraday". I have not established who made this annotation but it does not seem to be Faraday's own hand.

In each issue of the *Quarterly journal* there appeared a section entitled "Miscellaneous intelligence", which comprised reports of articles in other periodicals and short notes on experiments, etc. The latter sometimes have their author's name or initials appended, but the majority are anonymous. Fourteen such anonymous articles are ascribed to Faraday by the cumulative index.

There is no reason to doubt the accuracy of these ascriptions. Although I have not found any evidence to corroborate the manuscript annotation ascribing the compilation of the index to Faraday, it can be shown that Faraday was on occasion concerned in the editing of the *Quarterly journal of science*, and in particular of the Miscellaneous intelligence section. Moreover many of the anonymous items which the index ascribes to Faraday can be shown in other ways to be by Faraday.

W. T. Brande, Professor of Chemistry at the Royal Institution, was editor of the *Quarterly journal*, but seems on occasion to have delegated this duty to a subordinate. Brande's position as editor is made clear by an entry for January 8, 1816, in the Minute books of the Managers of the Royal Institution: "That Mr. Brande be requested to undertake the office of Editor [of the *Quarterly journal*] and to employ such assistants as he may find requisite."

S. P. Thompson in his *Michael Faraday: his life and work*, 1898, says (p. 76): "Faraday frequently wrote for it [the *Quarterly journal*] during these years [i.e. about 1816], and took editorial charge of it on more than one occasion during Brande's holidays."

In 1816 Faraday wrote: "When Mr. Brande left London in August [1816], he gave the *Quarterly journal* in charge to me: it has had very much of my time and care, and writing, through it, has been more abundant with me." (Bence-Jones, *Life and letters*. 2nd ed., 1870, vol. 1, p. 202–3).

In the *Quarterly journal* for January 1823 (vol. 14, pp. 435–36) there is a short article, Effect of cold on magnetic needles (no. 94) which is signed "Ed.". In the cumulative index 1–20 this article is ascribed to Faraday; it is also reprinted in *Experimental researches in electricity*, vol. 2.

S. P. Thompson in his *Michael Faraday* . . . , 1898, quotes (pp. 91–92) a letter from Faraday to De la Rive dated March 24, 1823. In it Faraday says that the results of his experiments on hydrate of chlorine "will appear in the next number of the *Quarterly Journal*, over which I have no influence". Brande had begun a course of lectures at the Royal Institution in February.

In the *Philosophical magazine* 1832, vol. 11, p. 236, there is the following editorial note: "Mr. Faraday, finding that he has been considered, both abroad and at home, as the Editor of the *Quarterly journal of science*, has requested us to state that he has never in any respect stood in that position, except in part for the Miscellanea only: that he deserves no praise for the good it may have done to science, and that, on the other hand, he is not responsible for anything but the papers and notices which bear his name or initials." The *Quarterly journal* had then just ceased publication.

Many of the anonymous items which the cumulative index ascribes to Faraday can be shown to be his by other means. In the *Quarterly journal* for 1818, vol. 4, p. 155 the article "Combustion of the diamond" (no. 21) is unsigned, but it is ascribed to Faraday in the cumulative index. It is also reprinted in *Experimental researches in chemistry and physics*. Other of these anonymous items are included amongst the material in the Faraday collection at the Royal Institution.

(2) Faraday's bookcase at the Royal Institution contains a collection of manuscripts and printed material concerning Sir Humphry Davy and Faraday which was given to the Institution by Faraday and his wife, Sarah. (See: *Notice of the proceedings at the meetings . . . of the Royal Institution, 1866–69*, vol. 5, pp. 193–94.) It includes Faraday's manuscript notes of lectures given at the Royal Institution and books bound by him.

The item in this collection with which we are now concerned is a volume entitled "Papers, notes, notices, etc., up to 1832". Some of the papers, etc., included are cut out from the periodical in which they appeared, others are in Faraday's manuscript. The volume is bound by Faraday. Printed items in this volume are noted in the bibliography when necessary as corroborating evidence of Faraday's authorship. All manuscript items are noted. The items are indicated as "In Faraday Collection" or "In Faraday Collection (in manuscript)".

Many of the items in this volume originally appeared anonymously and many of these are also ascribed to Faraday by the cumulative index to vols. 1–20 of the *Quarterly journal* (nos. 25–27, 30, 35–36, 41, 44, 57, 70, 74–75). A few are included in this volume which do not appear in the index (e.g. nos. 28, 38, 46).

PAPERS READ AT SOCIETIES, ETC.

The most important of these are those read before the Royal Society. Papers were also read at meetings of the British Association and of the Institution of Civil Engineers. For most of the items of this kind I have given references to the paper as published unabridged. References to abstracts and reports of papers are in general given only when no unabridged publication has been found. Where such abstracts or reports are by Faraday I have so indicated.

LECTURES

Faraday had a great reputation as a lecturer. Sir Frederick Pollock in his *Personal remembrances* (London, Macmillan, 1887) says (p. 248): "Amongst all the lecturers heard by me he [Faraday] was easily the first. . . . There was a peculiar charm and fascination about Faraday which placed him on an elevation too high for comparison with others." The obituary notice in *Chemical news* compares unfavourably the style of his early *Chemical manipulation* with that of his lectures: "The style in which it [*Chemical manipulation*] is written, although clear, is verbose, and far from elegant. This is the more remarkable, inasmuch as he was almost unrivalled as a lecturer, not only for his clearness, but conciseness, and the power of rousing the enthusiasm of his audience." (*Chemical news*, 1867, vol. 16, p. 111.) See also S. P. Thompson, *Michael Faraday*, 1898, p. 231–39.

But Faraday had little care to publish his lectures. A letter to W. Smith in answer to a proposed publication of the juvenile lectures of 1858–59 hints at reasons. It had been suggested that the lectures be taken down in shorthand. Faraday replied: ". . . even if I cared to give time to the revision of the mss. still the lectures without the experiments and the vivacity of speaking would fall far behind those in the lecture-room as to effect. And then I do not desire to give time to them, for money is no temptation to me. . . ." (Bence-Jones, *Life and letters*, 2nd ed., vol. 2, p. 418.)

The Christmas lectures for juveniles at the Royal Institution which were published when Faraday had achieved fame and popularity appeared through the initiatives of others. Sir William Crookes edited the lectures on the various forces of matter and those on the chemical history of a candle, J. Scoffern the lectures on the non-metallic elements.

In 1810 Faraday was introduced to the City Philosophical Society, which had been founded by a Mr. Tatum in 1808. This society consisted of thirty or forty young men who met for mutual instruction. Lectures were given once a fortnight by the members in turn. Faraday began to lecture there in January 1816 and continued until 1819. One of these lectures was printed (no. 13), and Bence-Jones gives extracts from some of them. All the lectures before the Society which Bence-Jones notices are included in the bibliography. Faraday's manuscripts for these lectures have recently been discovered by Dr. L. P. Williams.

In his lecture to the City Philosophical Society on February 19, 1817 (no. 13) Faraday refers to a portfolio in which the lectures delivered to the Society were preserved. I have found no trace of this portfolio.

In 1827 Faraday gave a course of lectures on chemical manipulation at the London Institution (no. 140). A syllabus of these lectures was printed (copies at Guildhall Library and the Royal Institution) but they were not otherwise published, although their substance was similar to that of *Chemical manipulation*, published in the same year (no. 153). This is indicated by a remark in the preface to *A catalogue of the Library of the London Institution . . . preceded by an historical and bibliographical account of the establishment*. 1835–43: ". . . In 1827 Mr. Faraday delivered a very interesting course of twelve lectures upon Chemical manipulation; in which were performed such of the processes described in his work on that subject, subsequently published,—as were capable of being explained to a general audience." (Vol. 1, Introductory preface, p. xxxi.)

As well as his numerous lectures at the Royal Institution and individual lectures elsewhere, Faraday was for over twenty years a lecturer at the Royal Military Academy, Woolwich. He also gave a course of fourteen lectures on electricity to medical students at St. George's Hospital, London (no. 244) in 1835. None of these lectures were published.

In recording the Friday evening discourses and other lectures which Faraday gave at the Royal Institution I have had access to the Minute books of the Managers of the Royal Institution. In finding reports of these lectures which appeared in the *Athenaeum* I have been helped by a list compiled by Miss D. K. Hutchinson of the Royal Institution. From 1851 abstracts of lectures (occasionally the lectures in full) appear in the *Proceedings of the Royal Institution*.

Entries in the bibliography for lectures are of three kinds:

(1) Lectures printed in full or edited from Faraday's notes, e.g. nos. 336, 351, 457 and 464.

(2) Abstracts. These are so indicated. Where the report or abstract is by Faraday this is also indicated. References to reports and abstracts are not in general given where the lecture has been published in full. Sometimes references to two or more abstracts are given. As it has not always been possible to see such abstracts together at the same time, I have not always been able to indicate whether the abstracts are the same reprinted or different. In general abstracts appearing in the *Athenaeum* are different from those of the *Literary gazette*. From 1851 onwards the *Athenaeum* reprints the abstracts from the *Proceedings of the Royal Institution*.

(3) Title only given. These are so indicated. Such entries are often for lectures which expound researches recently reported in a paper, e.g. no. 302.

There are also a number of printed handbills in the Faraday collection at the Royal Institution which give syllabi of courses of lectures. These have been included where they appear to be the fullest account in print, e.g. nos. 140, 307, 343 and 372.

SERMONS

Faraday was a member of the Sandemanian or Glasite sect, and on occasion preached before his church. (Bence-Jones, *Life and letters*, 2nd ed. vol. 2, pp. 99–101, which includes, p. 101, a reproduction of notes for a sermon.) Four sermons, or rather "fragmentary notes", are included in a pamphlet collection edited by Dr. James Rorie and entitled, *Select exhortations delivered to various Churches of Christ*, 1910 (no. 487). There are copies in the Birmingham Reference Library and at Queen's College, Dundee. Rorie was Resident Physician and Superintendent of the Dundee Royal Lunatic Asylum from 1860 to 1903, and also a lecturer at University College, Dundee. He collected material on the Glasites and his collection (not yet catalogued) is now in the Library of Queen's College, Dundee. The collection includes a manuscript volume of sermons by members of the sect, and it is extracts from this volume which Rorie published as *Select exhortations*. Neither in the published pamphlet nor in the manuscript volume does Rorie indicate how he came by these "fragmentary notes", as he calls them, of Faraday. All the Faraday sermons in the manuscript volume are included in the published pamphlet.

PARLIAMENTARY PAPERS

Some of Faraday's published work appears in Parliamentary papers. He was a member of or gave evidence before more than one Government commission, and held posts of scientific adviser to the Admiralty and to Trinity House. Bence-Jones quotes a letter in which Faraday says that he has had applications for advice "from the Admiralty, the Ordnance, the Home Office, the Woods and Forests, and other departments" (2nd ed., vol. 2, pp. 228ff.), and also gives summaries of work done for Trinity House (e.g. 2nd ed., vol. 2, pp. 87, 413–17).

It is difficult to say how much material was published as a result of these appointments and connections. Perhaps little was intended for publication. S. P. Thompson in his *Life* refers (p. 68) to "nineteen large portfolios full of manuscripts" as the result of Faraday's work for Trinity House. The reports for Trinity House which have been found in Parliamentary papers would hardly amount to nineteen pages.

There are difficulties in finding material in Parliamentary papers of the nineteenth century. The indexes are not good and complete sets of the Papers themselves are not readily available. There are no complete runs in Birmingham and I have not been able to make a thorough search of sets elsewhere.

"WILLIAM FARADAY"

In six items in this bibliography a mysterious William Faraday appears as the author (nos. 245, 344, 449, 395a, 459, and 471). This is a mistake for Michael. In four of the items (nos. 245, 449, 459, and 471) the circumstantial evidence is such as to amount to definite proof, apart from the fact that for three there is Bence-Jones' word that Michael Faraday was the author. In a fifth item (no. 344) the signature W. Faraday appears on a letter written from the Royal Institution. Dr. L. P. Williams suggests that the mistake arose from the 'M' in Faraday's signature being misread as 'Wm'.

The only William Faraday I have found was an uncle of Michael who died in 1791.

MATERIALS NOT INCLUDED IN THE BIBLIOGRAPHY

Two main classes of material are excluded:

(1) Personal and miscellaneous letters from Faraday appearing in collections of letters and in published books generally, e.g. Three letters to Charles W. Siemens, dated March to June 1862 in *A Collection of letters to Sir Charles William Siemens, 1823–1883*, 1953 (not in Bence-Jones). A letter, in facsimile manuscript, to C. W. Woolnough in Woolnough's *The whole art of marbling . . . 1881*. This work is dedicated to Faraday. There are also letters from Faraday in *The life of Richard Owen*, by Richard Owen. London, Murray, 1894, p. 258, and in *Personal recollections . . .* by Mary Somerville. London, 1874, pp. 292–93, the former being reprinted in *Notes and records of the Royal Society*, 1952, vol. 10, pp. 60–62. A letter to James Nasmyth appears in *James Nasmyth, engineer; an autobiography*. London, Murray, 1883, pp. 284–85, and three letters to H. C. Oersted in his *Correspondance. Publiée par M. C. Harding*, t. 2, 1920, pp. 322–23, 327–28.

It was considered to be unnecessary for this work to attempt a comprehensive survey of letters published in this way. Letters which have been published in periodicals, usually as separate items and as being of a historical interest, have in general been included, if only to prevent them falling into a more complete oblivion. Such letters are arranged by the date on which they were written.

(2) Manuscript material. Except for lecture notes at the Royal Institution this bibliography does not in general include manuscripts. I have thought it worth while, however, to give an indication here of manuscripts which I have come across during the course of this work. Dr. L. P. Williams has assembled a large collection of photocopies

of Faraday manuscripts and it is hoped that this more extensive list may be published. The following list is thus haphazard rather than extensive.

MSS. at Royal Institution

Where Faraday's lecture notes exist in the Faraday Collection I have indicated this in the bibliography. I have also noted mss. items which appear in "Papers, notes, notices, etc., up to 1832" (see p. xvii). These are the only manuscript items which are noted in the bibliography and it must be stressed that I have not inspected the bulk of the mss. items at the Royal Institution, which consist mainly of Faraday's laboratory note books and letters.

There is, however, a manuscript volume entitled, *A classbook for the reception of mental exercises instituted July 1818*. These "mental exercises" are essays, letters, poems, and the like and are the productions of a mutual improvement group consisting of Faraday, E. Deeble, E. Barnard, T. Deacon and J. Cordier. There are 47 contributions in the book almost all unascribed. They are written in various hands, including Faraday's, and are dated from August 1818 to August 1819. Each member of the group had the book in his charge for an allotted time, during which he was responsible for copying in contributions received from the members. Because of this it is not possible to say with certainty which of the contributions are Faraday's, although the initials M.F. have been added in pencil in another hand at the head of two essays, both in Faraday's hand, "On argument", dated August, 1818, and "A mathematical love letter", dated November, 1818. The volume was bequeathed to the Royal Institution by T. J. F. Deacon of Newcastle upon Tyne in 1901.

MSS. at British Museum

Letters to Charles Babbage, 1825–64. (Add. mss. 37182–37201).
Memoir of his life, 1835. Not autographed. (Add. mss. 40419, f. 81).
Letter to R. Brown, 1846. (Add. mss. 32, 441, f. 416).
Correspondence with Sir Robert Peel, 1846. (Add. mss. 40587, ff. 141, 143).
Letter to Sir Robert Owen, 1849. (Add. mss. 39954, f. 138).
Letter to R. Griffin, 1860. (Add. mss. 28, 510, f. 41).

Mss. in the archives of J. Wedgewood & Sons, Stoke-on-Trent

Three letters to J. Wedgewood, York Street, giving analysis of clays. Dated Royal Institution, February to March 1819.

Mss. at Royal Society, London

56 letters; 28 mss. papers published in the *Philosophical transactions*; 25 miscellaneous items.

Mss. at the Institution of Electrical Engineers

The Silvanus P. Thompson collection contains 34 autographic items, mostly letters on scientific matters, including 10 letters to Richard Phillips. (*Handlist of the . . . library of S. P. Thompson*, 1914, p. vii.) Also the Blaikley collection of Faraday mss.

Mss. at Trinity College Library, Cambridge

Correspondence between William Whewell and Faraday.

Mss. in Cavendish Laboratory Archives, Cambridge

Letters to Clerk Maxwell and drawings of lines of magnetic force. (*Notes and records of the Royal Society*, 1952, vol. 10, no. 2, pp. 139–47.)

Mss. at Royal Military Academy, Sandhurst

The letters received by the R.M.A. (then at Woolwich), 1829–46 include some from Faraday. These volumes of letters are not yet fully catalogued. (Information from the Librarian and from article by W. M. Roberts, "Michael Faraday at the Royal Military Academy", in *R.M.A. magazine*, July 1931.)

Mss. in Library of the American Philosophical Society

Letter to C. R. Weld of January 8, 1848 (no. 364). (Information from the Librarian.)

Mss. in Burndy Library, Norwalk, Connecticut

Letter to R. Phillips dated Brighton, November 29, 1831. (Given in Bence-Jones, *Life and letters*, vol. 2, pp. 6–10.)

Mss. at Trinity House, London

S. P. Thompson in his *Michael Faraday, his life and work*, 1898, refers (p. 68) to "nineteen large portfolios full of manuscripts" in which were the records of his work for Trinity House. These portfolios were given to Trinity House by Sarah Faraday (Bence-Jones, *Life and letters*, vol. 2, p. 92). Many of the documents at Trinity House were destroyed by fire in the last war and there is now no Faraday material there. (Information from Trinity House.)

Mss. at Public Record Office, London

Faraday became a member of the Scientific Committee of the Admiralty in January 1830. A cursory inspection of the Admiralty records in the P.R.O. for the period 1830–35 revealed three holograph letters of Faraday. There are probably more. As Faraday also did work for other government departments (see above, Parliamentary papers) this would seem to be a field in need of further research.

Mss. in Quetelet archives, Brussels

Seven letters to Adolphe Quetelet, dated between 1847 and 1865. (Notes on some unpublished letters from Faraday to Quetelet. By J. Pelseneer. *Annals of science*, 1936, vol. 1, pp. 447–52. Four of the letters are here reproduced.)

Mss. in Public University Library of Geneva

Correspondence with Gaspard and Auguste de la Rive, in all some 30 letters dated between 1818–61. (*Nature*, 1931, vol. 128, pp. 349–51.)

Mediumistic writings

A third class of excluded material may be mentioned here. Faraday seems to have inspired a small corpus of spiritualist literature. An example of this rubbish is *The evolution of the universe; or, Creation according to science. Transmitted from Michael Faraday, late electrician and chemist of the Royal Institution of London.* Los Angeles, Cosmos Publishing Co., 1924. (Copy at Library of Congress.) There are other publications of a like kind. Their titles, while sufficiently indicating the eccentricity of their content, fail to convey the full absurdity of their illustrations.

ARRANGEMENT OF ENTRIES

Entries are arranged chronologically. Where there is more than one entry for the same date the arrangement is alphabetical by title. It was thought that such arrangement would be helpful in giving some indication of the development of Faraday's thought.

Where the date of a lecture or of a paper read before a society can be ascertained, arrangement is according to this date and not according to the date of its first appearance in print.

Articles in periodicals (i.e. which are not also papers read or lectures) are arranged according to the month of publication of the relevant part of the periodical, as far as this could be ascertained. Such entries are arranged after the entries for particular dates in the month.

Books are listed according to the year in which they were published and are arranged at the end of monthly entries for the year. Also in this sequence are items for which a more precise dating in the year could not be established, such items being distinguished by an asterisk (*).

No attempt has been made to determine the precise date of publication for an item appearing as, or as part of, a Parliamentary paper. Such items are listed according to the date of the sessional volume in which they appear and are included in the entries after December.

Later issues and editions are listed immediately after the first, with references from their dates in the main sequence.

References to articles in periodicals give an abbreviated title of the periodical, the year, the volume number, the pagination and the date of issue, in that order. The full title of the periodical is given in the list of abbreviations.

Where an item appears in more than one publication, its earliest appearance is listed first. I have not attempted to find all the later appearances of articles and papers, etc.

Later editions of books are listed with the first edition and detailed descriptions are not repeated where they are identical with those preceding, omissions being indicated by three dots (. . .).

Parliamentary papers bring their own problems of description and mode of reference. It is often difficult to decide what constitutes the title of a Parliamentary paper, for there may be differences between the title on the paper cover and the title-page, or between the short and long form of the title. For a discussion of such complexities see the *Select list of British Parliamentary papers, 1833–99*, by P. and G. Ford, 1953, pp. ix–xii.

Command, or session and paper numbers, are the decisive means of identifying Parliamentary papers. All references to these papers are to sets of House of Commons sessional papers. They are preceded by the abbreviation *Parl. pap.* and are in accordance with the rules given by Hansard in his Alphabetical index, 1801–26:

"References in this index are made 1st to the Year or Session in which the paper was printed; 2nd to the Printer's number of the Paper, as printed at the bottom of the page; 3rd to the volume of the Sessional set in which such Paper is contained."

For the period with which we are concerned square brackets were used for Command papers to distinguish them from House papers, but unfortunately the Command numbers were not printed on the paper. Page numbers are given where appropriate to denote parts of an individual paper. They refer to the page numbers of that paper, not to any pagination of the sessional volume.

ACKNOWLEDGEMENTS

The compiler expresses his sincere thanks to all who have helped in the preparation of this bibliography:

Mr. K. D. C. Vernon, Librarian of the Royal Institution, and his assistant, Mr. A. J. Horne, who have unfailingly given encouragement and advice at all stages, and at whose suggestion this bibliography was undertaken. In addition, Mr. Vernon has devoted much time and energy to seeing the work through the press, and Mr. Horne has given valuable help in the preparation of the index.

Dr. L. Pearce Williams of Cornell University, who first drew my attention to the bibliography by Mme Lukomskaya, and who has readily given help and advice on many occasions.

The Lenin State Library, Moscow, and the Institute for the History of Science and Technology of the Academy of Sciences, U.S.S.R., who generously furnished copies of Mme Lukomskaya's bibliography.

Mr. F. C. Francis, Director and Principal Librarian of the British Museum, for advice in preparing the original version of this bibliography, which was submitted in part requirement for the Diploma in Librarianship of the University of London.

Mr. D. W. Doughty of Queen's College, Dundee, University of St. Andrews; Lt.-Col. G. A. Shepherd of the Central Library, Royal Military Academy, Sandhurst; the Secretary of the Senate of the University of London.

The following libraries and institutions: the Admiralty, London; the American Philosophical Society; the Birmingham Reference Library; the British Museum; the Faraday Society; the Guildhall Library, London; the Institution of Civil Engineers and the Institution of Electrical Engineers; the Pratt Institute, Brooklyn; the Public Record Office, London; the Royal Society, London; St. George's Hospital Medical School, London; Southwark Public Libraries; Trinity College Library, Cambridge; Trinity House, London.

Messrs. J. M. Dent Ltd., Bernard Quaritch, Ltd., and Chatto and Windus Ltd.

My colleagues at Birmingham, and finally my wife, to whom is the greatest debt of all.

It remains to add that for the inevitable errors and omissions the compiler remains responsible, and would be grateful if these could be brought to his attention.

A. E. J.

Birmingham University Library,
1959.

BIOGRAPHICAL REFERENCES

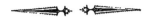

The following are the main biographies of Faraday:

Andrews, Percy Edgar: *Michael Faraday, 1791–1867*. (Makers of history series no. 13.) Exeter, A. Wheaton, 1937.

Appleyard, Rollo: *A tribute to Michael Faraday*. London, Constable, 1931.

Ashcroft, E. W.: *Faraday*. London, British Electrical and Allied Manufacturers Assocn., 1931.

Bence-Jones, Henry: *The life and letters of Faraday*. 2 v. London, Longmans, Green, 1870. The first edition of Bence-Jones has 50 pages of matter omitted from the second edition, also published in 1870.

Bragg, Sir William Henry: *Michael Faraday*. (Broadcast national lectures no. 8.) London, British Broadcasting Corporation, 1931. [A broadcast talk on March 4, 1931. Reprinted in *Scientific Monthly*, 1931, **33**, 481–99.]

Burgess, William Roscoe: *Michael Faraday*. London, Wesleyan Conference Office [1877].

Cohn, Emil: *Faraday und Maxwell*. (Deutsches Museum. Abhandlungen und Berichte, **4**, 1.) Berlin, V.D.I. Verlag, 1932.

Cramp, William: *Michael Faraday and some of his contemporaries*. London, Pitman, 1931.

Crowther, James Arnold: *The life and discoveries of Michael Faraday*. (Pioneers of Progress. Men of Science. Ed. by S. Chapman.) London, Society for Promoting Christian Knowledge, 1918.

Dibner, Bern: *Faraday discloses electro-magnetic induction. His epochal letter sent from Brighton to Richard Phillips, F.R.S. is here reproduced*. (Burndy Library publication, no. 5.) New York, Burndy Library, 1949.

Gladstone, John Hall: *Michael Faraday*. London, Macmillan, 1872. 2nd ed., 1873.

Hadfield, *Sir* Robert Abbott: *Faraday and his metallurgical researches, with special reference to their bearing on the development of alloy steels*. London, Chapman and Hall, 1931.

Jarrold, Walter: *Michael Faraday: man of science*. London, S. W. Partridge [1891].

Kendall, James: *Michael Faraday: man of simplicity*. London, Faber, 1955.

Martin, Thomas: *Faraday*. (Great lives, no. 40.) London, Duckworth, 1934.

Martin, Thomas: *Faraday's discovery of electro-magnetic induction*. London, E. Arnold, 1949.

Naccari, Andrea: *La vita di Michele Faraday*. Padova, Fratelli Drucker, 1908.

Ostwald, Wilhelm: *Michael Faraday; eine psychographische Studie* . . . Zurich (etc.), Roscher, [1924].

Randall, Wilfred L.: *Michael Faraday, 1791–1867*. (Roadmaker series.) London, L. Parsons; Boston, Small, Maynard, 1924.

BIOGRAPHICAL REFERENCES

Riley, James Frederic: *The hammer and the anvil: a background to Michael Faraday.* Clapham, via Lancaster, Yorkshire, Dalesman Publishing Co., 1954.

Thompson, Silvanus Phillips: *Michael Faraday: his life and work.* (Century science series.) London, Cassell, 1898. Reprinted 1901.

Tyndall, John: *Faraday as a discoverer.* London, Longmans, Green, 1868. [Originally published in *R.I. Proc.* 1866–69, **5**, 199–272 as two lectures given at the R.I. on January 17 and 24, 1868.] New eds. 1870 and 1877. 4th ed., 1884. 5th ed., 1894.

In addition to the above books the various obituary notices which were published in periodicals and newspapers about the time of Faraday's death in 1867 are valuable because they express the views of his contemporaries.

Numerous articles on Faraday and various aspects of his life and work were published about the time of the Centenary of Faraday's discovery of electro-magnetic induction in 1931. Similarly, the centenaries of his birth in 1891 and his discovery of benzene in 1925 led to further publications in journals.

LIST OF ABBREVIATIONS

Ann. chim.	*Annales de chimie*. Paris. New series, **1–75**: 1816–40; new series **1–69**: 1841–63.
Ann. elec.	*The annals of electricity, magnetism and chemistry*. . . . Conducted by William Sturgeon. London. **1–10**: 1836–43.
Ann. phil.	*Annals of philosophy, or magazine of chemistry, mineralogy, mechanics natural history, agriculture and the arts*. By Thomas Thomson. London. **1–16**: 1813–20; series 2, **1–12** (also as **17–28**): 1821–26.
Ath.	*Athenaeum (and literary chronicle)*. . . . London. 1828–.
Bibl. univ.	*Bibliothèque universelle des sciences, belles-lettres et arts, faisant suite à la bibliothèque britannique rédigee à Genève. Partie des sciences*. Genève. **1–60**: 1816–35; nouvelle série, **1–60**: 1836–45.
Bibl. univ. Arch.	*Archives des sciences physiques et naturelles; supplément à la bibliothèque universelle et revue suisse*. Genève. **1–36**: 1846–57.
B-J	Bence-Jones, Henry. *The life and letters of Faraday*. 2nd ed. 2 v. London, Longmans, Green, 1870. *Note:* References are given in the same form as for periodicals, e.g. B-J **2**: 1–6 means v. 2 pages 1–6.
Brit. Assoc. rep.	British Association for the Advancement of Science. *Report of the . . . meetings . . . , 1831–*. 1833–. *Note:* The references in the bibliography are to the date of the meeting.
Chem. gaz.	*The chemical gazette*. . . . London. **1–17**: 1842–59.
Chem. news	*The chemical news* . . . London. **1–**: 1860 (i.e. December 10, 1859)–.
Civ. eng.	*The civil engineer and architects' journal*. London. **1–31**: 1837–68.
Comptes rendus de l'Acad. Sci.	*Comptes rendus hebdomadaires des séances de l'Académie des Sciences*. . . . Paris. Tome 22, janvier-juin 1846.
Edin. phil. j.	*The Edinburgh philosophical journal*. . . . Edinburgh. **1–14**: 1819–26.
Edin. new phil. j.	*The Edinburgh new philosophical journal*. . . . Edinburgh. **1–57**: 1826–54; new series, **1–19**: 1855–64.
Elec. mag.	*The electrical magazine*. London. **1–2**: 1843–46.
F.	Used throughout the bibliography to indicate Faraday.
J. chem. ed.	*Journal of chemical education*. Easton. **26**: 1949.
J. Chem. Soc.	*Journal of the Chemical Society*. London. **28** (also as new series, **13**): 1875.

J. Soc. Arts	*Journal of the Society of Arts.* London. **7**: 1858–59.
Lit. gaz.	*Literary gazette. . . .* London. 1817–62.
Lond. med. gaz.	*London medical gazette.* London. **1–48** (**36–48** also as new series, **1–13**): 1827–51.
Mech. mag.	*The mechanics' magazine. . . .* London. **1**–: 1823–.
Min. proc. Instn. Civ. Engrs.	*Minutes of proceedings of the Institution of Civil Engineers, with abstracts of the discussions.* London. **1**–: 1837–.
n.d.	no date in imprint.
n.p.	no place of publication in imprint.
Pall Mall gaz.	*Pall Mall gazette.* London. **7**: 1868.
Parl. pap.	Great Britain. Parliamentary papers. (House of Commons series.)
Pharm. j.	*Pharmaceutical journal and transactions.* London. **15**: 1855–56.
Phil. mag.	*The philosophical magazine and journal. . . .* London. **43–68**: 1814–26; *The philosophical magazine, or annals of chemistry. . . .* **1–11**: 1827–32; *The London and Edinburgh philosophical magazine. . . .* **1–16**: 1832–40; *The London, Edinburgh, and Dublin philosophical magazine.* **17–37**: 1840–50; new series, **1**–: 1851–.
Phil. trans.	*Philosophical transactions of the Royal Society.* London.
Photog. Soc. j.	*Journal of the Photographic Society of London.* London. **6**: 1860.
Quart. j. sci.	*Journal of science and the arts; ed. at the Royal Institution.* London. **1–6**: 1816–19; *Quarterly journal of science, literature and the arts,* **7–22**: 1819–27 (i.e. December 1826) (**7** has title, *Quarterly journal of literature, science and the arts*); new series **1–7** (but without volume numbering): 1827–30.
Rep. pat. invent.	*The repertory of patent inventions, and other discoveries and improvements. . . .* London. Enlarged series, **1–5**: 1843–45.
R.I.	Royal Institution of Great Britain.
R.I. proc.	*Notices of the proceedings at the meetings of the members of the Royal Institution, with abstracts of the discourses delivered at the evening meetings.* London. **1**–: 1851–.
Roy. Inst. j.	*Journal of the Royal Institution of Great Britain.* London. **1–2**: 1831.
Roy. Soc. proc.	*Abstracts of the papers printed in the Philosophical transactions of the Royal Society of London from 1800 to 1843.* London. **1–4**: 1832–43; *Abstracts of the papers communicated to the Royal Society . . . 1843–1854.* **5–6**: 1851–54; *Proceedings of the Royal Society . . . 1854–.* **7**–: 1856–.
Trans. Newcomen Soc.	*The transactions of the Newcomen Society.* London. **3**: 1922–23.
Yrbk. facts	*Arcana of science. . . .* By John Timbs. London. 1828–38; *The yearbook of facts in science and arts. . . .* By John Timbs. 1839–.

* Distinguishes items for which no date within a year could be established. (See Introduction p. xxiii.)

MICHAEL FARADAY

A LIST OF HIS LECTURES AND PUBLISHED WRITINGS

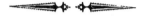

MICHAEL FARADAY

1816

1 On the general properties of matter.
> Extracts in *B-J* **1**: 191–92.
> F's first lecture at the City Philosophical Society, Jan. 17.

2 On the attraction of cohesion.
> Title only in *B-J* **1**: 191.
> F's second lecture at the City Philosophical Society, April 10, 1816.

3 Analysis of the native caustic lime [of Tuscany].
> *Quart. j. sci.* 1816, **1**: 261–62 (July).
> Reprinted in *Experimental researches in chemistry and physics*.

4 Some account of the alstenia teiformis, or tea of Bogota. Drawn up from the Journal of M. Palacio Faxar.
> *Quart. j. sci.* 1817, **2**: 92–94 (Oct. 1816).

*5 On chemical affinity.
> Extracts in *B-J* **1**: 192–93.
> F's third lecture at the City Philosophical Society.

*6 On radiant matter.
> Extracts in *B-J* **1**: 193–96.
> F's fourth lecture at the City Philosophical Society.

*7 On oxygen, chlorine, iodine, fluorine.
> Extracts in *B-J* **1**: 196–98.
> F's fifth lecture at the City Philosophical Society.

*8 On hydrogen.
> Extracts in *B-J* **1**: 198–99.
> F's sixth lecture at the City Philosophical Society.

*9 On nitrogen.
> Title only in *B-J* **1**: 191.
> F's seventh lecture at the City Philosophical Society.

10   Notice of some experiments on flame made by Sir H. Davy.

       Quart. j. sci. 1817, **2**: 463–64 (Jan.).
       Signed M.F.

11   On the wire-gauze safe-lamps.

       Quart. j. sci. 1817, **2**: 464–65 (Jan.).
       Signed M.F.

12   Report on some experiments made with compressed oxygene and hydrogene, in the laboratory of the Royal Institution.

       Quart. j. sci. 1817, **2**: 461–62 (Jan.).
       Signed M.F.

13   Some observations on the means of obtaining knowledge, and on the facilities afforded by the constitution of the City Philosophical Society. Read to the body of members at 53, Dorset Street, Salisbury Square, February 19, 1817. London, Effingham Wilson, 1817.

       (3), 6–15 pp. 21·5 cm.
       A part of this Lecture is given in *B-J* **1**: 210–12.

14   Some experiments and observations on a new acid substance [formed from ether].

       Quart. j. sci. 1817, **3**: 77–81 (April).

*15   On the atmosphere.

       Title only in *B-J* **1**: 208.
       F's eighth lecture in his chemical series at the City Philosophical Society.

*16   On sulphur and phosphorus.

       Title only in *B-J* **1**: 208.
       F's ninth lecture in his chemical series at the City Philosophical Society.

17   On carbon.

       Title only in *B-J* **1**: 209.
       F's tenth lecture in his chemical series at the City Philosophical Society, given on July 16.
       For this lecture F. used notes; in previous lectures he had written out all he intended to say.

18   An account of some experiments on the escape of gases through capillary tubes.

       Quart. j. sci. 1817, **3**: 354–55 (July).
       Reprinted in *Experimental researches in chemistry and physics*.

*19   On combustion.

       Title only in *B-J* **1**: 209.
       F's eleventh lecture in his chemical series at the City Philosophical Society.

20 On the metals generally.

> Title only in *B-J* 1: 209.
>
> F's twelfth lecture in his chemical series at the City Philosophical Society, Oct. 15, 1817.

21 Combustion of the diamond.

> *Quart. j. sci.* 1818, **4**: 155 (Oct. 1817).
>
> Unsigned, but ascribed to F. in index 1–20 (*see* Introduction pp. xv–xvii), and reprinted in *Experimental researches in chemistry and physics*.

22 Effects of inhaling the vapour of sulphuric ether.

> *Quart. j. sci.* 1818, **4**: 158–59 (Oct. 1817).
>
> Unsigned, but noted in F's copy of *Experimental researches in chemistry and physics* in the library of the Institution of Electrical Engineers (*see* Introduction p. xv).

1818

23 On the solution of silver in ammonia.

> *Quart. j. sci.* 1818, **4**: 268–73 (Jan.).
>
> Reprinted in *Experimental researches in chemistry and physics*.

24 On the sulphuret of phosphorus.

> *Quart. j. sci.* 1818, **4**: 361–62 (Jan.).

25 Change of colour by acids.

> *Quart. j. sci.* 1818, **5**: 125 (April).
>
> Unsigned, but in Faraday Collection and ascribed to F. in index 1–20.

26 Changes of colour by heat.

> *Quart. j. sci.* 1818, **5**: 128–30 (April).
>
> Unsigned, but in Faraday Collection and ascribed to F. in index 1–20.

27 Chromic oxide and acid.

> *Quart. j. sci.* 1818, **5**: 124 (April).
>
> Unsigned, but in Faraday Collection and ascribed to F. in index 1–20.

28 Cocoa nut oil.

> *Quart. j. sci.* 1818, **5**: 124 (April).
>
> Unsigned, but in Faraday Collection.

29 On some combinations of ammonia with chlorides.

> *Quart. j. sci.* 1818, **5**: 74–77 (April).
>
> Reprinted in *Experimental researches in chemistry and physics*.

30 Strength of ale. [Report of an analysis by W. T. Brande.]

> *Quart. j. sci.* 1818, **5**: 124 (April).
>
> Unsigned, but in Faraday Collection and ascribed to F. in index 1–20.

31   Observations on the inertia of the mind.

> Extracts in *B-J* **1**: 230–44.
>
> See also article by Fraser-Harris, "A little-known discourse by F.", *Discovery*, 1931, **12**: 311–13.
>
> A lecture at the City Philosophical Society on July 1.

32   On the sounds produced by flame in tubes, etc.

> *Quart. j. sci.* 1818, **5**: 274–80 (July).
>
> Article dated May 11, 1918.
>
> Reprinted in *Experimental researches in chemistry and physics*.

33   Reduction of the oxide of silver by ammonia.

> *Quart. j. sci.* 1818, **5**: 368–69 (July).
>
> Signed M.F. and in Faraday Collection.

34   Account of a chemical analysis of French plate paper, India yellow paper, and India white paper. (*In: Practical hints on decorative printing with illustrations engraved on wood, and printed in colours at the type press*. By William Savage. London, 1822, pp. 80–84.)

> In form of letter to Savage dated R.I. Oct. 8, 1818.

35   Benzoates. Benzoates of mercury.

> *Quart. j. sci.* 1819, **6**: 159 (Oct. 1818).
>
> Unsigned, but in Faraday Collection and ascribed to F. in index 1–20.

36   Benzoates of iron.

> *Quart. j. sci.* 1819, **6**: 159–60 (Oct. 1818).
>
> Unsigned, but in Faraday Collection and ascribed to F. in index 1–20.

37   Benzoates of zinc.

> *Quart. j. sci.* 1819, **6**: 160 (Oct. 1818).
>
> Signed M.F. and in Faraday Collection.

38   Benzoic acid.

> *Quart. j. sci.* 1819, **6**: 152 (Oct. 1818).
>
> Unsigned, but in Faraday Collection.

39   Boracic acid.

> *Quart. j. sci.* 1819, **6**: 152 (Oct. 1818).
>
> Signed M.F.
>
> Reprinted in *Experimental researches in chemistry and physics*.

40   Hydrometer.

> *Quart. j. sci.* 1819, **6**: 133–34 (Oct. 1818).
>
> Signed M.F. and in Faraday Collection.

- perfect barriers to chemical action
× Induction on a globe and Electrometers
× Through a plate of mica or glass – thus accumulate
× Feather hung up in a jar
× Leyden jar – battery d. their power.

There is nothing more extraordinary in Electricity than the power of conveying it which some bodies have – Conduction

× Remains on glass. Conical jar and pith balls.
× —————— globe hung by silk
× But touch the globe with metal and effects cease
× Very long wire and arrangements for conduction
The conduction is instantaneous

×. Discharge a jar by the long wire – rate of passage as never been determined – but according to Wheatstone is at at 400 feet in $\frac{1}{10000}$ of a second or 4000000 feet in a second

Nothing looks more like a transmission of something than this; yet is not at all divisive – Compare it to sound and also to light × Transmission of sound along a rod. This due to mere mechanical force × then their forces in Chladnis forms on plates

The flash or spark is another form of electricity in which seems independent of other bodies altogether

×. Spark – Conductor of heat – jar – Battery
× In long exhausted tube – There the power seems to have

I. A TYPICAL PAGE FROM ONE OF FARADAY'S LECTURE NOTEBOOKS

41 Muriate of zinc.
> *Quart. j. sci.* 1819, **6**: 159 (Oct. 1818).
> Unsigned, but in Faraday Collection and ascribed to F. in index 1–20.

42 Observations on gallic acid, tannin, etc.
> *Quart. j. sci.* 1819, **6**: 154–56 (Oct. 1818).

43 On sirium, or vestium.
> *Quart. j. sci.* 1819, **6**: 112–15 (Oct. 1818).

44 Pure spring water [in Lord Harewood's park in Yorkshire].
> *Quart. j. sci.* 1819, **6**: 171 (Oct. 1818).
> Unsigned, but in Faraday Collection (in manuscript) and ascribed to F. in index 1–20.

45 Separation of iron and manganese.
> *Quart. j. sci.* 1819, **6**: 153–54 (Oct. 1818).
> Signed M.F. and in Faraday Collection.

46 Tartrate of potash and manganese.
> *Quart. j. sci.* 1819, **6**: 158 (Oct. 1818).
> Unsigned, but in Faraday Collection.

47 Triple tartrates of bismuth.
> *Quart. j. sci.* 1819, **6**: 158 (Oct. 1818).
> Signed M.F. and in Faraday Collection.

*48 On gold, silver, mercury, etc.
> Extracts in *B-J* **1**: 222–23.
> F's thirteenth lecture in his chemical series at the City Philosophical Society.

*49 On copper and iron.
> Title only in *B-J* **1**: 221.
> F's fourteenth lecture in his chemical series at the City Philosophical Society.

*50 On tin, lead, zinc.
> Title only in *B-J* **1**: 221.
> F's fifteenth lecture in his chemical series at the City Philosophical Society.

*51 On antimony, arsenic.
> Extracts in *B-J* **1**: 223–26.
> F's sixteenth lecture in his chemical series at the City Philosophical Society.

*52 On alkalies and earths.
> Extracts in *B-J* **1**: 226–29.
> F's seventeenth and concluding lecture in his chemical series at the City Philosophical Society.

53 Carburetted hydrogen.

> *Quart. j. sci.* 1819, **6**: 358–60 (Jan.).
> Signed M.F. and in Faraday Collection.

54 Manganese.

> *Quart. j. sci.* 1819, **6**: 358 (Jan.).
> Signed M.F. and in Faraday Collection.

55 Nitrous oxide.

> *Quart. j. sci.* 1819, **6**: 360–61 (Jan.).
> Signed M.F. and in Faraday Collection.

56 Separation of manganese from iron.

> *Quart. j. sci.* 1819, **6**: 357–58 (Jan.).
> Signed M.F.

57 Gunpowder inflamed without a spark.

> *Quart. j. sci.* 1819, **7**: 183 (April).
> Unsigned, but in Faraday Collection and ascribed to F. in index 1–20.

58 Some experimental observations on the passage of gases through tubes.

> *Quart, j. sci.* 1819, **7**: 106–10 (April).
> Reprinted in *Experimental researches in chemistry and physics.*

59 Analysis of a stone used in the setting of fine cutlery.

> *Quart. j. sci.* 1819, **7**: 399–400 (July).
> Included in Faraday Collection (in manuscript).

60 An analysis of Wootz, or Indian steel.

> *Quart. j. sci.* 1819, **7**: 288–90 (July).
> Dated April 14th, 1819.
> Reprinted in Hadfield, Sir Robert A., *Faraday and his metallurgical researches*, 1931, pp. 81–83.

61 On sirium, or vestium.

> *Quart. j. sci.* 1819, **7**: 291–93 (July).

62 Palm wine.

> *Quart. j. sci.* 1819, **7**: 387–88 (July).
> Signed M.F.
> In Faraday Collection (in manuscript).

63 Pyrometrical gauge [for a wind furnace].

> *Quart. j. sci.* 1819, **7**: 384–85 (July).
> Signed M.F. and in Faraday Collection (in manuscript).
> A manuscript note by F. in his own copy of *Experimental researches in chemistry and physics* (now in library of Institution of Electrical Engineers) refers to this article as "Pneumatic chimney gauge".

64   Strength of Aetna wines.

> *Quart. j. sci.* 1820, **8**: 168 (Oct. 1819).
> Signed M.F. and in Faraday Collection (in manuscript).

*65   On the forms of matter.

> Extracts in *B-J* **1**: 265–73.
> A lecture at the City Philosophical Society.

1820

66   On the decomposition of chloride of silver, by hydrogen, and by zinc.

> *Quart. j. sci.* 1820, **8**: 374–76 (Jan.).
> Reprinted in *Experimental researches in chemistry and physics.*

67   Soda alum.

> *Quart. j. sci.* 1820, **8**: 386 (Jan.).
> Signed M.F.

68   Facts respecting the increased volatility and inflammability which fish oil and its vapours acquire by continued or renewed exposure to certain high temperatures; elicited by the examination of evidence in a late trial in the Court of Common Pleas, Severn, King and co. versus Drew, or the Imperial Insurance Office, before the Lord Chief Justice Dallas and a special jury.

> *Phil. mag.* 1820, **55**: 252–89 (F's testimony, pp. 280 and 282.)
> A report of the proceedings at the trial which took place April 11–13.
> *See also* no. 69.

69   Observations on the chemical part of the evidence, given upon the late trial of the action brought by Messrs. Severn, King and co., against the Imperial Insurance Co. By Samuel Parkes.

> *Quart. j. sci.* 1821, **10**: 340–43, 350–51 (F's evidence).
> *See also* no. 68.

70   Preservation of crystals.

> *Quart. j. sci.* 1820, **9**: 185 (April).
> Unsigned, but in Faraday Collection and ascribed to F. in index 1–20.

71   Description of a new apparatus for the combustion of the diamond.

> *Quart. j. sci.* 1820, **9**: 264–65 (July).
> Signed M.F.
> Reprinted in *Experimental researches in chemistry and physics.*

72 Experiments on the alloys of steel, made with a view to its improvement. By Faraday and James Stodart.

> *Quart. j. sci.* 1820, **9**: 319–30 (July).
> *Phil. mag.* 1820, **56**: 26–35 (July).
> *Phil. mag.* 1822, **60**: 335*–62*.
> *Edin. phil. j.* 1820, **3**: 308–12 (=pp. 325–30 of *Quart. j. sci.* supra).
> Reprinted in *Experimental researches in chemistry and physics.*

73 Lettre au Prof. de la Rive sur les alliages que forme l'acier avec différens métaux.

> *Bibl. univ.* 1820, **14**: 209–15 (no. 3, July).
> Dated R.I. 26 Juin 1820.
> This letter given in English in *B-J* **1**: 291–97.

74 Red fire.

> *Quart. j. sci.* 1820, **9**: 411 (July).
> Unsigned, but in Faraday Collection (in manuscript), and ascribed to F. in index 1–20.

75 Test for baryta and strontia.

> *Quart. j. sci.* 1821, **10**: 189 (Oct. 1820).
> Unsigned, but in Faraday Collection (in manuscript), and ascribed to F. in index 1–20.

76 On two new compounds of chlorine and carbon, and on a new compound of iodine, carbon and hydrogen.

> *Phil. trans.* 1821: 47–74 (read Dec. 21, 1820).
> *Ann. phil.* 1821, **2**: 104–20.
> *Phil. mag.* 1822, **59**: 337–53.
> Reprinted in *Experimental researches in chemistry and physics.*

1821

77 On the vapour of mercury at common temperatures.

> *Quart. j. sci.* 1821, **10**: 354–55 (Jan.).
> Reprinted in *Experimental researches in chemistry and physics.*

78 Letter to Ampère.

> *Trans. Newcomen Soc.* 1922/23, **3**: 119–21, with facsimile of one page on plate xxi.
> Dated R.I. 1821, Feb. 2.
> Article states that this letter is preserved in the Darmstaedter Collection of the Staatsbibliothek at Berlin. It is not included in Bence-Jones.
> Reprinted in *Correspondance du Grand Ampère.* Edited by L. de Launay. Paris, 1936–43, pp. 909–11.

79 Dissection of crystals.

> *Quart. j. sci.* 1821, **11**: 202 (April).
> Signed M.F. and in Faraday Collection.

80 On a new compound of chlorine and carbon. By Faraday and R. Phillips.

> *Phil. trans.* 1821: 392–97 (read July 12, 1821).
> *Phil. mag.* 1822, **59**: 33–36.
> Reprinted in *Experimental researches in chemistry and physics.*

81 Letter to R. Phillips. (*In: A letter to Mr. Samuel Parkes, occasioned by his observations on the oil question. By Richard Phillips.*)

> *Quart. j. sci.* 1821, **11**: 333 (July).
> Letter dated R.I. June 5, 1821.

82 Singular property of boracic acid.

> *Quart. j. sci.* 1821, **11**, 403–04 (July).
> Signed M.F.
> Reprinted in *Experimental researches in chemistry and physics.*

83 Historical sketch of electro-magnetism.

> *Ann. phil.* 1821, **2**: 195–200, 274–90; 1822, **3**: 107–21 (Sept. 1821–Feb. 1822).
> Unsigned. F. acknowledged authorship of these articles in *Quart. j. sci.* 1823, **15**: 290–91, and in a letter to *Ann. phil.* 1823, **6**: 67.

84 Contact in voltaic electricity.

> *Quart. j. sci.* 1822, **12**: 185 (Oct. 1821).
> Signed M.F. and in Faraday Collection.

85 New electro-magnetic apparatus.

> *Quart. j. sci.* 1822, **12**: 186–87 (Oct. 1821).
> Signed M.F. and in Faraday Collection.
> Reprinted in *Experimental researches in electricity*, v. **2**.

86 On some new electro-magnetical motions, and on the theory of magnetism.

> *Quart. j. sci.* 1822, **12**: 74–96 (Oct. 1821).
> Dated Sept. 11, 1821.
> Reprinted in *Experimental researches in electricity*, v. **2**.

1822

87 Description of an electro-magnetical apparatus for the exhibition of rotatory motion.

> *Quart. j. sci.* 1822, **12**: 283–85 (Jan.).
> Reprinted in *Experimental researches in electricity*, v. **2**.

88 Note on new electro-magnetical motions.

> *Quart. j. sci.* 1822, **12**: 416–21 (Jan.).
> Reprinted in *Experimental researches in electricity*, v. **2**.

89   On the alloys of steel. By Faraday and James Stodart.

> *Phil. trans.* 1822: 253–70 (read March 21).
> *Edin. phil. j.* 1822, **7**: 350–63.
> *Phil. mag.* 1822, **60**: 363–74.
> *Ann. phil.* 1823, **5**: 199–209.
> Reprinted in *Experimental researches in chemistry and physics.*

90   Hydriodide of carbon.

> *Quart. j. sci.* 1822, **13**: 429 (July).
> Signed M.F.
> Reprinted in *Experimental researches in chemistry and physics.*

91   On the changing of vegetable colours as an alkaline property, and on some bodies possessing it.

> *Quart. j. sci.* 1822, **13**: 315–17 (July).
> Reprinted in *Experimental researches in chemistry and physics.*

91a Letter to Ampère, dated R.I. [September 3, 1822].

> *Correspondance du Grand Ampère.* Edited by L. de Launay. Paris, 1836–43, pp. 928–29.

92   Action of salts on turmeric paper.

> *Quart. j. sci.* 1823, **14**: 234 (Oct. 1822).
> Reprinted in *Experimental researches in chemistry and physics.*

93   Evidence before Select Committee on roads from London to Holyhead, etc., in the year 1822. (*In: Fifth report of the Select Committee . . . pp.* 180–83, 189–95.)

> *Parl. pap.* 1822 (417) vi.
> F. gave evidence on May 13 and June 1, 1822. His evidence on June 1 included a letter dated R.I. May 7.

1823

94   Effect of cold on magnetic needles.

> *Quart. j. sci.* 1823, **14**: 435–36 (Jan.).
> Signed Ed. Ascribed to F. in index 1–20, in Faraday Collection (*see* Introduction pp. xvi–xvii), and reprinted in *Experimental researches in electricity,* v. **2**.

95   Letter to G. D. Yeats. (*In: Some hints on a mode of procuring soft water at Tunbridge Wells. . . . By* G. D. Yeats.)

> *Quart. j. sci.* 1823, **14**: 347 (Jan.).

96   New electro-magnetic experiments [by Sebeck].

> *Quart. j. sci.* 1823, **14**: 442 (Jan.).
> Signed Ed. F. edited this issue of *Quart. j. sci.* (*See* no. 94.)

97 On the temperature produced by vapour, and on the temperature of vapour.

> *Quart. j. sci.* 1823, **14**: 439–41 (Jan.).
> *Ann. phil.* 1823, **5**: 74–75 (Jan.), with title, "On the temperature produced by the condensation of vapour". Both abstracts of *Ann. chim.* 1822, **20**: 320–25.

98 On fluid chlorine.

> *Phil. trans.* 1823: 160–64 (read March 13).
> *Phil. mag.* 1823, **62**: 413–15.
> *Ann. phil.* 1824, **7**: 89–91.
> Reprinted in *Experimental researches in chemistry and physics,* and in *The liquefaction of gases* (Alembic Club reprint, no. 12) (no. 483).

99 On the condensation of several gases into liquids.

> *Phil. trans.* 1823: 189–98 (read April 10).
> *Edin. phil. j.* 1823, **9**: 381–84.
> *Phil. mag.* 1823, **62**: 416–23.
> *Ann. phil.* 1824, **7**: 93–97 (included in, "On the liquefaction of chlorine and other gases).
> Reprinted in *Experimental researches in chemistry and physics,* and in *The liquefaction of gases* (Alembic Club reprint, no. 12) (no. 483).

100 On hydrate of chlorine.

> *Quart. j. sci.* 1823, **15**: 71–74 (April).
> There is an additional (editorial) note at p. 163.
> Reprinted in *Experimental researches in chemistry and physics.*

101 Historical statement respecting electro-magnetic rotation.

> *Quart. j. sci.* 1823, **15**: 288–92 (July).
> In Faraday Collection with ms. note by F., "this shown to Wollaston before being printed who made some pencil alterations and declared it to be 'perfectly satisfactory'." The copy so corrected is bound with F's copy of his papers from *Phil. trans.* at R.I.
> Reprinted in *Experimental researches in electricity,* v. **2**.

102 Action of gunpowder on lead.

> *Quart. j. sci.* 1823, **16**: 163 (Oct.).
> Signed M.F.
> *Ann. phil.* 1823, **6**: 396.
> Reprinted in *Experimental researches in chemistry and physics.*

103 Change of musket balls in Shrapnell shells.

> *Quart. j. sci.* 1823, **16**: 163 (Oct.).
> Signed M.F.
> *Ann. phil.* 1823, **6**: 395–96
> Reprinted in *Experimental researches in chemistry and physics.*

104 Purple tint of plate glass affected by light.

> *Quart. j. sci.* 1823, **16**: 164 (Oct.).
> Signed M.F.
> *Ann. phil.* 1823, **6**: 396.
> Reprinted in *Experimental researches in chemistry and physics.*

114   On some cases of the formation of ammonia, and on the means of testing the presence of minute portions of nitrogen in certain states.

       Quart. j. sci. 1825, **19**: 16–26 (April).

       Reprinted in *Experimental researches in chemistry and physics.*

115   On the substitution of tubes for bottles, in the preservation of certain fluids, such as chloride of sulphur, protochlorides of phosphorus, and carbon, etc.

       Quart. j. sci. 1825, **19**: 149–50 (April).

       Signed M.F. and reprinted in *Experimental researches in chemistry and physics.*

116   On new compounds of carbon and hydrogen, and on certain other products obtained during the decomposition of oil by heat.

       Phil. trans. 1825: 440–66 (read June 16).
       Ann. phil. 1826, **11**: 44–50, 95–104.
       Phil. mag. 1825, **66**: 180–97.

       Reprinted in *Experimental researches in chemistry and physics.*

117   Colour of glass as affected by light.

       Quart. j. sci. 1825, **19**: 341–42 (July).

       Signed M.F.

118   Composition, etc., of formic acid.

       Quart. j. sci. 1825, **19**: 355 (July).

       Signed M.F.

119   Electric powers of oxalate of lime.

       Quart. j. sci. 1825, **19**: 338–39 (July).

       Signed M.F. and reprinted in *Experimental researches in electricity,* v. **2.**

120   Electro-magnetic current.

       Quart. j. sci. 1825, **19**: 338 (July).

       Signed M.F. and reprinted in *Experimental researches in electricity,* v. **2.**

121   Plan of an extended and practical course of lectures and demonstrations on chemistry, delivered in the laboratory of the Royal Institution, by William Thomas Brande, and M. Faraday.

       Quart. j. sci. 1826, **20**: [203–4].

       Two courses were given, the first began on Oct. 11, 1825, the second on Feb. 14, 1826.

*122   Electro-magnetic rotations.

       Title only in *B-J* **1**: 346.

       Ms. notes at R.I.

       After his appointment as Director of the Laboratory at the R.I., Faraday "invited members of the Institution to come to evening meetings in the laboratory. '3 or 4 meetings took place this year.'" (*B-J* supra.) This was one of them. The Friday Evening discourses developed from these meetings.

123　On pure caoutchouc.

> Title only in *B-J* **1**: 350.
> Ms. notes at R.I.
> Lecture at R.I., Feb. 3 (cf. no. 129).

124　On Brunel's condensed gas-engine.

> *Quart. j. sci.* 1826, **21**: 131–32.
> Report of lecture at R.I. on Feb. 10.
> Ms. notes at R.I.

125　On the mutual action of sulphuric acid and naphthaline, and on a new acid produced.

> *Phil. trans.* 1826: 140–62 (read Feb. 16).
> *Ann. phil.* 1826, **12**: 201–15.
> Reprinted in *Experimental researches in chemistry and physics.*

126　Lithography: the general theory of the processes.

> *Quart. j. sci.* 1826, **21**: 133–34.
> Report of lecture at R.I. on March 3.
> Ms. notes at R.I.

127　On a limit to the production of vapour.

> *Quart. j. sci.* 1826, **21**: 324.
> Abstract (by F.) of lecture at R.I. on April 7.
> Unsigned, but in Faraday Collection.
> *Ann. phil.* 1826, **11**: 390–91.
> Another report.

128　Bi-sulphuret of copper.

> *Quart. j. sci.* 1826, **21**: 183 (April).
> Signed M.F. and in Faraday Collection.

129　On pure caoutchouc, and the substances by which it is accompanied in the state of sap or juice.

> *Quart. j. sci.* 1826, **21**: 19–28 (April).
> Reprinted in *Experimental researches in chemistry and physics.*

130　On hydro-carbon and sulphuric acid.

> *Quart. j. sci.* 1826, **21**: 330–32.
> Abstract (by F.) of lecture at R.I. on May 5.
> Unsigned, but in Faraday Collection.
> Ms. notes at R.I.

131 On Drummond's geodesical station light.

> *Quart. j. sci.* 1826, **21**: 332–33.
> Abstract (by F.) of lecture at R.I. on May 12.
> Unsigned, but in Faraday Collection.
> *Ann. phil.* 1826, **11**: 453.
> Another report.
> Ms. notes at R.I.

132 On Brunel's tunnel at Rotherhithe.

> *Quart. j. sci.* 1826, **21**: 335–36.
> Abstract (by F.) of lecture at R.I. on June 9.
> Unsigned, but in Faraday Collection.
> Ms. notes at R.I.

133 On the existence of a limit to vaporization.

> *Phil. trans.* 1826: 484–93 (read June 15).
> *Ann. phil.* 1826, **12**: 436–41.
> Reprinted in *Experimental researches in chemistry and physics.*

134 Crystallization of sulphur.

> *Quart. j. sci.* 1826, **21**: 392–93 (July).
> *Ann. phil.* 1826, **12**: 148.
> Unsigned, but in Faraday Collection.

135 Fluidity of sulphur at common temperatures.

> *Quart. j. sci.* 1826, **21**: 392 (July).
> Signed M.F.
> *Ann. phil.* 1826, **12**: 390–91.
> Reprinted in *Experimental researches in chemistry and physics.*

136 Plan of an extended and practical course of lectures and demonstrations on chemistry, delivered in the laboratory of the Royal Institution by W. T. Brande and M. Faraday.

> *Quart. j. sci.* 1827, **22**: [231–32].
> Two courses were given, the first began on Oct. 10, 1826, the second on Feb. 13, 1827.

137 On a peculiar perspective appearance of aerial light and shade.

> *Quart. j. sci.* 1827, **22**: 81–83 (Oct. 1826).
> Signed M.F.
> Reprinted in *Experimental researches in chemistry and physics.*

138 On the confinement of dry gases over mercury.

> *Quart. j. sci.* 1827, **22**: 220–21 (Oct. 1826).
> Signed M.F.
> *Ann. phil.* 1826, **12**: 388–89.
> Reprinted in *Experimental researches in chemistry and physics.*

139 A general account, accompanied with experimental illustrations, of the late extension of our knowledge relative to magnetism, founded on the discovery of M. Arago, of the effects of metal when in motion.

> *Quart. j. sci.* 1827 [n.s. **1**]: 209–10.
> Abstract of lecture at R.I. on Jan. 26.
> *Phil. mag.* 1827, **1**: 231.
> Another abstract.
> Ms. notes at R.I.

140 London Institution. 1827. Prospectus of Mr. Faraday's lectures on the philosophy and practice of chemical manipulation. February 13–May 8.

> Handbill. 32 × 18 cm.
> A course of 12 lectures. Short extract in *B-J* **1**: 354–56.
> Ms. notes at R.I.

141 Measurements and weight of a sea-gull.

> *Quart. j. sci.* 1827 [n.s. **1**]: 244 (March).
> Unsigned, but in Faraday Collection (in manuscript).

142 On the probable decomposition of certain gaseous compounds of carbon and hydrogen, during sudden expansion.

> *Quart. j. sci.* 1827 [n.s. **1**]: 204–6 (March).
> Unsigned, but reprinted in *Experimental researches in chemistry and physics*.

143 On some general points of chemical philosophy.

> Short extracts in *B-J* **1**: 353–54.
> A course of 6 (?) lectures at the R.I. beginning April 28.
> Ms. notes at R.I.
> *Note:* Managers' minutes at R.I. give four lectures on chemical philosophy, begun April 27. Ms. notes and *B-J* indicate six lectures, the ms. notes giving April 28 as date for commencement.

144 On the chemical action of chlorine and its compounds as disinfectants [title from ms. notes].

> *Quart. j. sci.* 1827 [n.s. **1**]: 460–62.
> Abstract (by F.) of lecture at R.I. on May 4.
> Unsigned, but in Faraday Collection.
> *Phil. mag.* 1827, **1**: 467–68.
> Another report.
> Ms. notes at R.I.

145 On the progress and present state of the Thames Tunnel.

> *Quart. j. sci.* 1827 [n.s. **1**]: 466.
> Report of lecture at R.I. on June 15.
> *Lit. gaz.* 1827: 410 (June 30).
> Another report.
> *Phil. mag.* 1827, **2**: 68.
> Another and shorter report.
> Ms. notes at R.I.

Royal Institution of Great Britain,

ALBEMARLE STREET,

December 3, 1827

A

COURSE OF SIX ELEMENTARY LECTURES

ON

CHEMISTRY,

ADAPTED TO A JUVENILE AUDIENCE, WILL BE DELIVERED
DURING THE CHRISTMAS RECESS,

BY MICHAEL FARADAY, F.R.S.

Corr. Mem. Royal Acad. Sciences, Paris ; Director of the Laboratory, &c. &c.

The Lectures will commence at Three o'Clock.

Lecture I. Saturday, December 29. Substances generally—
Solids, Fluids, Gases—Chemical affinity.

Lecture II. Tuesday, January 1, 1828. Atmospheric Air and
its Gases.

Lecture III. Thursday, January 3. Water and its Elements.

Lecture IV. Saturday, January 5. Nitric Acid or Aquafortis—
Ammonia or Volatile Alkali—Muriatic Acid or Spirit of Salt—
Chlorine, &c.

Lecture V. Tuesday, January 8. Sulphur, Phosphorus, Carbon,
and their Acids.

Lecture VI. Thursday, January 10. Metals and their Oxides—
Earths, Fixed Alkalies and Salts, &c.

———

Non-Subscribers to the Institution are admitted to the above
Course on payment of One Guinea each ; Children 10*s.* 6*d.*

[Turn over.

146 Transference of heat by change of capacity in gas.

> *Quart. j. sci.* 1827 [n.s. **1**]: 474–75 (June).
> *Phil. mag.* 1827, **2**: 230.
>
> Unsigned, but reprinted in *Experimental researches in chemistry and physics*.

146a Corrections in a work entitled Chemical manipulation.

> *Phil. mag.* 1827, **2**: 58 (July).
>
> Corrects errors in paras. 139 and 265. (*See* No. 153.)

146b Letter to Ampère, dated R.I., September 5, 1827.

> *Correspondance du Grand Ampère.* Edited by L. de Launay. Paris, 1936–43, p. 947.

147 Lectures and demonstrations in theoretical and practical chemistry, commencing 9th Oct., 1827, by Brande and Faraday.

> *Quart. j. sci.* 1827 [n.s. **2**]: 4.
>
> Notice only, "Prospectus obtained by application".
> Two courses were given, the second began Feb. 12, 1828.

148 Description of two remarkable ores of copper from Cornwall. By William Phillips. With analysis of the same, by M. Faraday.

> *Phil. mag.* 1827, **2**: 286–89 (Oct.).
>
> F. contributed two paragraphs, "Examination of the Condurrite", and "Examination of the arsenuriet of copper".

149 Experiments on the nature of Labarraque's disinfecting soda liquid.

> *Quart. j. sci.* 1827 [n.s. **2**]: 84–92 (Oct.).
>
> Reprinted in *Experimental researches in chemistry and physics*.

150 Faraday's Chemical manipulations.

> *Quart. j. sci.* 1827 [n.s. **2**]: 221 (Oct.).
>
> Signed M.F.
> Short note correcting an error in paras. 599 and 600. (*See* no. 153.)

151 A course of six elementary lectures on chemistry, adapted to a juvenile audience . . . by Michael Faraday. . . .

> *Quart. j. sci.* 1827 [n.s. **2**]: viii.
>
> A lecture prospectus.
> Christmas lectures at R.I. Dec. 29, 1827 to Jan. 10, 1828.
> Ms. notes at R.I. The same notes were used for the Christmas lectures of 1837–38. (*See* no. 274.)

152 On the fluidity of sulphur and phosphorus at common temperatures.

> *Quart. j. sci.* 1827 [n.s. **2**]: 469–70 (Dec.).
> *Phil mag.* 1828, **3**: 144–45.
>
> Reprinted in *Experimental researches in chemistry and physics*.

153   Chemical manipulation; being instructions to students in chemistry, on the methods of performing experiments of demonstration or of research, with accuracy and success. London, printed and published by W. Phillips, George-yard, Lombard-street; sold also by W. Tait, Edinburgh; and Hodges and McArthur, Dublin, 1827.

> (viii) (x) 11–656 pp. illus. 22 cm.
>
> Reviewed in: *Quart. j. sci.* 1827 [n.s. **2**]: 275–83; *Phil. mag.* 1827, **2**: 58–66; *Lit. gaz.* 1827: 472–73 (July 21).

1829

Chemical manipulation . . . John Murray, 1829.

> Copy not seen. Listed in Sotheran catalogue, no. 800, 1926, as 2nd issue of 1st ed.

1830

Chemical manipulation . . . New ed. London, John Murray, Albemarle-street, 1830.

> (xii) 646 pp. illus. 23 cm.
>
> ". . . In the present edition I have made many corrections and alterations, without enlarging the book. . . ." Preface.

1842

Chemical manipulation . . . 3rd ed., revised. London, John Murray, Albemarle-street, 1842.

> (2) (xiv) 664 pp. illus. 23 cm.

1828

154   Illustrations of the new phenomena produced by a current of air or vapour recently observed by M. Clementi [title from ms. notes].

> *Quart. j. sci.* 1828 [n.s. **3**]: 168–71.
>
> Report (by F.) of a lecture at R.I. on Feb. 1.
>
> Unsigned, but in Faraday Collection and noted in F's copy of *Experimental researches in chemistry and physics* at I.E.E.
>
> *Phil. mag.* 1828, **3**: 229 (another report).
>
> Ms. notes at R.I.

155   Chemical lectures and demonstrations by Brande and Faraday, commencing 12th February 1828.

> *Quart. j. sci.* 1827 [n.s. **2**]: viii.
>
> Notice only, "Prospectus on application".

156   General account of vibrations producing sound [title from ms. notes].

> *Lit. gaz.* 1828: 137–38 (March 1).
> *Phil. mag.* 1828, **3**: 230.
> *Quart. j. sci.* 1828 [n.s. **3**]: 173.
> Various reports of lecture at R.I. on Feb. 15.
> Ms. notes at R.I.

(156) Supplementary remarks on the reciprocation of sound.
> *Lit. gaz.* 1828: 169 (March 15).
> *Phil. mag.* 1828, **3**: 304.
> *Quart. j. sci.* 1828 [n.s. **3**]: 417.
> Various reports of lecture at R.I. on March 7.
> Ms. notes at R.I.
> F. delivered these two lectures from material supplied by C. Wheatstone.

157 Anhydrous crystals of sulphate of soda.
> *Quart. j. sci.* 1828 [n.s. **3**]: 223–24 (March).
> Signed M.F.
> Reprinted in *Experimental researches in chemistry and physics*.

158 On the relation of water to hot polished surfaces.
> *Quart. j. sci.* 1828 [n.s. **3**]: 221–22 (March).
> Signed M.F. and in Faraday Collection.

159 On the operations of the laboratory.
> *Quart. j. sci.* 1828 [n.s. **3**]: 439–40.
> A prospectus for a series of eight lectures, April 19 to June 7.
> Ms. notes at R.I.

160 Nature of musical sound.
> *Lit. gaz.* 1828: 329–30 (May 24).
> *Phil. mag.* 1828, **3**: 457.
> *Quart. j. sci.* 1828 [n.s. **3**]: 424–26.
> Various reports of lecture at R.I. on May 9 from material supplied by C. Wheatstone.
> Ms. notes at R.I.

161 Thames tunnel; its recent and present state [title from ms. notes].
> *Phil. mag.* 1828, **4**: 65.
> *Quart. j. sci.* 1828 [n.s. **3**]: 436.
> Reports of lecture at R.I. on June 13.
> Ms. notes at R.I.

1829

162 An account of Mr. Brown's discovery of active molecules existing in solid bodies, either organic or inorganic.
> *Lit. gaz.* 1829: 127 (Feb. 21).
> *Phil. mag.* 1829, **5**: 230–31.
> *Quart. j. sci.* 1829 [n.s. **5**]: 363–65.
> Various reports of lecture at R.I. on Feb. 13.
> Ms. notes at R.I.

163 Brard's test of the action of weather on building materials.

> *Lit. gaz.* 1829: 160 (March 7).
> *Phil. mag.* 1829, **5**: 307.
> *Quart. j. sci.* 1829 [n.s. **5**]: 371–72.
> Various reports of lecture at R.I. on Feb. 27.
> Ms. notes at R.I.

164 On Mr. Wheatstone's illustrations of the resonance or reciprocated vibrations of volumes of air.

> *Lit. gaz.* 1829: 241 (April 11).
> *Phil. mag.* 1829, **5**: 390–91.
> *Quart. j. sci.* 1829 [n.s. **5**]: 379–80.
> Various reports of a lecture at R.I. on April 3.
> Ms. notes at R.I.

165 A course of six lectures at R.I. on various points of chemical philosophy, May 2–June 6.

> *B-J* **1**: 361, "His subjects were, water, hydrocarbons, artificial heat, artificial light, safety lamp, common salt."
> Ms. notes at R.I.

166 Brunel's block machine.

> *Lit. gaz.* 1829: 320 (May 16).
> *Phil. mag.* 1829, **6**: 70.
> *Quart. j. sci.* 1829 [n.s. **5**]: 381–82.
> Various reports of lecture at R.I. on May 8.
> Ms. notes at R.I.

167 On the nodal figures of vibrating surfaces.

> *Lit. gaz.* 1829: 361 (May 30).
> *Phil. mag.* 1829, **6**: 70.
> *Quart. j. sci.* 1829 [n.s. **5**]: 382–84.
> Various reports of a lecture delivered for C. Wheatstone at R.I. on May 22.
> Ms. notes at R.I.

168 On the manufacture of glass for optical purposes.

> *Lit. gaz.* 1829: 408–9 (June 20).
> *Phil. mag.* 1829, **6**: 70–71.
> *Quart. j. sci.* 1829 [n.s. **5**]: 390–91.
> Various reports of a lecture at R.I. on June 12.
> *See also* no. 170.
> Ms. notes at R.I.

169 Electricity of the solar rays. Letter from Carlo Mattrucci [i.e. Matteuci] of Forli, to Prof. Gazzeri.

> *Quart. j. sci.* 1829 [n.s. **6**]: 173–74 (Sept.).
> A short note, signed M.F., is appended.

170 On the manufacture of glass for optical purposes.

> *Phil. trans.* 1830: 1–57 (Bakerian lecture, read Nov. and Dec. 1829).
> Reprinted in *Experimental researches in chemistry and physics.*

171 A course of elementary lectures on electricity, Dec. 29, 1829 to Jan. 9, 1830.

> *B-J* **1**: 363.
> Ms. notes at R.I.
> Christmas juvenile lectures 1829–30.

See 153 Chemical manipulation . . . John Murray, 1829.

1830

172 On Aldini's method of protection for men exposed to flame by use of asbestos [title from ms. notes].

> *Lit. gaz.* 1830: 73–74 (Jan. 30).
> *Phil. mag.* 1830, **7**: 211–12.
> *Quart. j. sci.* 1830 [n.s. **7**]: 175–76.
> Various reports of lecture at R.I. on Jan. 22.
> Ms. notes at R.I.

173 Transmission of musical sounds through solid conductors and their ultimate reciprocation [title from ms. notes].

> *Ath.* 1830: 154–55 (no. 124, March 13).
> *Lit. gaz.* 1830: 223–24 (April 3).
> *Phil. mag.* 1830, **7**: 316.
> *Quart. j. sci.* 1830 [n.s. **7**]: 190.
> Various reports of lecture delivered for C. Wheatstone at R.I. on March 5.
> Ms. notes at R.I.

174 On the flowing of sand under pressure.

> *Ath.* 1830: 266–67 (no. 131, May 1).
> *Lit. gaz.* 1830: 288–89 (May 1).
> *Phil. mag.* 1830, **8**: 68.
> Various reports of lecture at R.I. on April 23.
> Ms. notes at R.I.

175 On the geodetical survey of Ireland in progress under Col. Colby [title from ms. notes].

> *Ath.* 1830: 297–98 (no. 133, May 15).
> *Lit. gaz.* 1830: 336–37 (May 22).
> *Phil. mag.* 1830, **8**: 68–69.
> Various reports of lecture at R.I. on May 7.
> Ms. notes at R.I.

176 On the application of a new principle in the construction of musical instruments.

> *Ath.* 1830: 330–31 (no. 135, May 29).
> *Lit. gaz.* 1830: 369–70 (June 5).
> *Phil. mag.* 1830, **8**: 69.
> *Quart. j. sci.* 1830 [n.s. **7**]: 397–98.
> Various reports of lecture delivered for C. Wheatstone at R.I. on May 21.
> Ms. notes at R.I.

177 On the laws of co-existing vibrations in strings and rods.

> *Ath.* 1830: 378–79 (no. 138, June 19).
> *Lit. gaz.* 1830: 401 (June 19).
> *Phil. mag.* 1830, **8**: 70–71.
> *Quart. j. sci.* 1830 [n.s. **7**]: 405–6.
> Various reports of lecture delivered for C. Wheatstone at R.I. on June 11.
> Ms. notes at R.I.

178 On the limits of vaporisation.

> *Roy. Inst. j.* 1831, **1**: 70–76 (Oct. 1830).
> Reprinted in *Experimental researches in chemistry and physics.*

See 153 Chemical manipulation. New ed. 1830.

1831

179 On a peculiar class of optical deceptions.

> *Roy. Inst. j.* 1831, **1**: 205–23.
> Lecture at R.I. on Jan. 21.
> [Supplementary] note by M.F.
> *Roy. Inst. j.* 1831, **1**: 334–36.
> Reprinted in *Experimental researches in chemistry and physics.*
> Ms. notes (of lecture) at R.I.

180 On oxalamede.

> *Ath.* 1831: 139 (no. 174, Feb. 26).
> *Lit. gaz.* 1831: 136 (Feb. 26).
> Reports of lecture at R.I. on Feb. 18.
> Ms. notes at R.I.

181 Clement's experiment—easy mode of repeating it.

> *Roy. Inst. j.* 1831, **1**: 369 (Feb.).
> Signed M.F.

182 On the power of electricity to confer phosphorescence on certain metals.

> *Ath.* 1831: 218–19 (no. 179, April 2).
> *Lit. gaz.* 1831: 217 (April 2).
> *Phil. mag.* 1831, **9**: 381.
> Various reports of lecture at R.I. on March 25.
> Ms. notes at R.I.

183   Four lectures on chemical and natural philosophy, 14 April–5 May.

>   *Roy. Inst. j.* 1831, **1**: [iv].
>   Ms. notes at R.I.
>   April 14—optical deceptions; April 21—lithography; April 28—flowing of sand; May 5—caout-chouc. (From ms. notes.)

184   On Mr. Trevelyan's recent experiments on the production of sound during the conduction of heat.

>   *Roy. Inst. j.* 1831, **2**: 119–22.
>   Abstract (by F.) of lecture at R.I. on April 29.
>   Reprinted in *Experimental researches in chemistry and physics.*
>   Ms. notes at R.I.

185   On a peculiar class of acoustical figures, and on certain forms assumed by groups of particles upon vibrating elastic surfaces.

>   *Phil. trans.* 1831: 299–340 (read May 12, with appendix dated July 30).
>   Reprinted in *Experimental researches in chemistry and physics.*
>   cf. no. 186.

186   On the arrangements assumed by particles on the surfaces of vibrating elastic bodies.

>   *Ath.* 1831: 397–98 (no. 190, June 18).
>   *Lit. gaz.* 1831: 394–95 (June 18).
>   *Roy. Inst. j.* 1831, **2**: 130–31.
>   Various reports of lecture at R.I. on June 10.
>   Ms. notes at R.I.
>   cf. no. 185.

187   Experimental researches in electricity. [First series] 1. On the induction of electric currents. 2. On the evolution of electricity from magnetism. 3. On a new electrical condition of matter. 4. On Arago's magnetic phenomena.

>   *Phil. trans.* 1832: 125–62 (read Nov. 24, 1831).
>   *See also* no. 297.

188   Letter to Hachette on F's researches in electricity, communicated to l'Académie des Sciences by Hachette on Dec. 26.

>   Report in *Le Temps*, Dec. 28.
>   Reprinted in *Ann. chim.* 1831, **48**: 402–3.
>   See S. P. Thompson, *Michael Faraday*, 1898, pp. 265–67 for the misunderstanding which arose from this "unfortunate" letter.

*189   Four lectures on geology.

>   R.I. Managers' minutes indicate F. as having given these lectures in 1831. No other reference to them found. Mistake for no. 183?

190 On the alleged decline of science in England. By a Foreigner [i.e. Gerrit Moll]. London, T. and T. Boosey, 1831.

> (4) 33 pp. 20·5 cm.
>
> Preface by Faraday, who published this pamphlet at his own expense (*see* no. 485, *Letters of Faraday and Schoenbein*, 1899, p. 62). BM catalogue says edited by F.

1833
(Another ed.)

1832

191 Experimental researches in electricity. 2nd series. 5. Terrestrial magneto-electric induction. 6. Force and direction of magneto-electric induction generally.

> *Phil. trans.* 1832: 163–94 (Bakerian lecture, read Jan. 12).
> *See also* no. 297.

192 On the Planariae.

> *Lit. gaz.* 1832: 74–75 (Feb. 4).
> *Lond. med. gaz.* 1832, **9**: 723–24 ⎫
> *Edin. new phil. j.* 1833, **28**: 183–85 ⎬ the same.
> *Phil. mag.* 1832, **11**: 299.
> Various reports of lecture at R.I. on Jan. 27.
> Ms. notes at R.I.

193 On the first two parts of his recent researches in electricity: volta-electric induction, and magneto-electric induction.

> *Lit. gaz.* 1832: 119 (Feb. 25).
> *Lond. med. gaz.* 1832, **9**: 839–40.
> *Phil. mag.* 1832, **11**: 300–1.
> Various reports of lecture at R.I. on Feb. 17.
> Ms. notes at R.I.
> cf. nos. 187 and 191.

194 On the explanation of Arago's phaenomena of moving metals by magneto-electric induction.

> *Lit. gaz.* 1832: 169 (March 17).
> *Phil. mag.* 1832, **11**: 462.
> Reports of lecture at R.I. on March 2.
> Ms. notes at R.I.
> cf. no. 187.

195 Letter deposited at Royal Society on a theory of progressive magnetism.

> *Royal Society occasional notices*, 1937, **2**: 9.
> *Wireless world*, 1938, **42**: 400–1 (May 5).
> Dated R.I. March 12, 1832.
> R.I.

196 Terrestrial magneto-electric induction [title from ms. notes].

> *Lit. gaz.* 1832: 217 (April 7).
> *Phil. mag.* 1832, **11**: 465–66.
> Reports of lecture at R.I. on March 30.
> Ms. notes at R.I.
> cf. no. 191.

197 *Quarterly journal of science.*

> *Phil. mag.* 1832, **11**: 236 (March).
> Note, at F's request, by editors of *Phil. mag.* that F. never editor of *Quart. j. sci. See* Introduction p. xvi (quoted in full).

198 Crispations of fluids [title from ms. notes].

> *Lit. gaz.* 1832: 329 (May 26).
> *Lond. med. gaz.* 1832, **10**: 300 (no. 235, June 2).
> *Phil. mag.* 1832, **1**: 74.
> Various reports of lecture at R.I. on May 18.
> Ms. notes at R.I.
> cf. no. 185.

199 On Mordan's apparatus for manufacturing Bramah's locks [title from *Lond. med. gaz.*].

> *Lit. gaz.* 1832: 361 (June 9).
> *Lond. med. gaz.* 1832, **10**: 432 (no. 239, June 30).
> *Phil. mag.* 1832, **1**: 75.
> Various reports of lecture at R.I. on June 1.

200 Syllabus of a course of five lectures upon some points of domestic chemical philosophy . . . 2nd June–30th June.

> Handbill. 21·5 × 15 cm.
> Lectures were on the candle, lamp, chimney, kettle and ashes.
> Report of last lecture in *Lit. gaz.* 1832: 425 (July 7).
> Ms. notes at R.I. (not those on kettle).
> *B-J* prints notes for lecture on kettle, **2**: 124–25.

201 On the new fowling piece of Wilkinson and Moser.

> *Lit. gaz.* 1832: 378 (June 16).
> Report of lecture at R.I. on June 8.

202 On the electro-motive force of magnetism. By Signori Nobili and Antinori; from the *Antologia*, no. 131: with notes by Michael Faraday.

> *Phil. mag.* 1832, **11**: 402–13 (June).
> Reprinted in *Experimental researches in electricity*, v. **2**.

203 New experiments relative to the action of magnetism on electro-dynamic spirals, and a description of a new electro-motive battery. By Signor Salvatore dal Negro; with notes by Michael Faraday.

> *Phil. mag.* 1832, **1**: 45–49 (July).
> Reprinted in *Experimental researches in electricity*, v. **2**.

204 Account of an experiment in which chemical decomposition has been effected by the induced magneto-electric current. By P.M.; preceded by a letter from Michael Faraday.

> *Phil. mag.* 1832, **1**: 161–62 (Aug.).
> Letter dated R.I. July 27.

205 Lettre à M. Gay-Lussac sur l'électro-magnétisme.

> *Ann. chim.* 1832, **51**: 404–34 (Oct. ?)
> English version in: *Phil. mag.* 1840, **17**: 281–89, 356–66.
> Reprinted in *Experimental researches in electricity*, v. **2**, with title, "Nobili and Antinori's errors in magneto-electric induction . . .".

206 Six lectures on chemistry.

> *Lit. gaz.* 1833: 11 (Jan. 5).
> Brief notice only. Noted in R.I. Managers' minutes.
> Christmas juvenile lectures, begun on Dec. 29.

1833

207 Experimental researches in electricity. 3rd series. 7. Identity of electricities derived from different sources. 8. Relation by measure of common and voltaic electricity.

> *Phil. trans.* 1833: 23–54 (read Jan. 10 and 17).
> *Phil. mag.* 1833, **3**: 162–71, 253–62, 353–62.
> *See also* no. 297.

208 On the identity of electricity derived from different sources [title from ms. notes].

> *Ath.* 1833: 90 (no. 276, Feb. 9).
> *Lit. gaz.* 1833: 89 (Feb. 9).
> *Phil. mag.* 1833, **2**: 312.
> Various reports of lecture at R.I. on Feb. 1.
> Ms. notes at R.I.
> cf. no. 207.

209 Report of Committee appointed by the Royal Society to examine the Proof standard for alcohol.

> F. a member of this Committee and presented its report on Feb. 12, 1833. It was appointed in 1832.
> Mentioned by C. E. S. Phillips, "Laboratory and platform; work for the state," in *The Times* Faraday number, Sept. 21, 1931, p. vii.

210 On the practical prevention of dry rot in timber; being the substance of a lecture delivered by Professor Faraday at the Royal Institution, February 22, 1833. With observations, etc. London, J. and C. Adlard, printers, Bartholomew Close, 1833.

> 24 pp. 20 cm.
>
> Reports appeared in *Phil. mag.* 1833, **2**: 313–14; *Lit. gaz.* 1833: 136 (March 2), and *Ath.* 1833: 139 (no. 279, March 2).
>
> Ms. notes at R.I.
>
> cf. no. 247.

> *1836*
> On the practical prevention of dry rot. . . . With observations, etc. London, John Weale, 1836.
>
> > 30 pp. 20 cm.

> *1837*
> (Another ed.)
>
> > 30 (2) pp. 21 cm.

211 Investigation of the velocity and other properties of electric discharges [title from ms. notes].

> *Ath.* 1833: 155 (no. 280, March 9).
> *Lit. gaz.* 1833: 152 (March 9).
>
> Reports of lecture at R.I. on March 1 from material supplied by C. Wheatstone.
>
> Ms. notes at R.I.

212 Address delivered at the commemoration of the centenary of the birth of Dr. Priestley.

> *Phil. mag.* 1833, **2**: 390–91.
>
> Commemoration was held at Freemasons' Hall, London, March 25.

213 On Mr. Brunel's new mode of building arches [title from ms. notes].

> *Ath.* 1833: 220 (no. 284, April 6).
> *Lit. gaz.* 1833: 217 (April 6).
>
> Reports of lecture at R.I. on March 29.
>
> Ms. notes at R.I.

214 On the mutual relations of lime, carbonic acid and water [title from ms. notes].

> *Ath.* 1833: 299 (no. 289, May 11).
> *Lond. med. gaz.* 1832–33, **12**: 191–92.
>
> Abstracts of a lecture at R.I. on May 3.
>
> Ms. notes at R.I.

215   Experimental researches in electricity. 4th series. 9. On a new law of electric conduction. 10. On conducting power generally.

> *Phil. trans.* 1833: 507–22 (read May 23).
> *See also* no. 297.

216   On a new law of electric conduction [title from ms. notes].

> *Lit. gaz.* 1833: 345 (June 1).
> *Lond. med. gaz.* 1832–33, **12**: 479.
> Abstracts of lecture at R.I. on May 24.
> Ms. notes at R.I.
> cf. no. 215.

217   A course of six lectures on electricity and magnetism, May to June.

> *B-J* **2**: 47, "His subjects were Common Electricity, Voltaic Electricity, Thermo-Electricity; Common Magnetism, Electro-Magnetism, Magneto-Electricity".

218   Experimental researches in electricity. 5th series. 11. On electro-chemical decomposition.

> *Phil. trans.* 1833: 675–710 (read June 20).
> *See also* nos. 221 and 297.

219   Notice of a means of preparing the organs of respiration, so as considerably to extend the time of holding the breath; with remarks on its application, in cases in which it is required to enter an irrespirable atmosphere, and on the precautions necessary to be observed in such cases.

> *Phil. mag.* 1833, **3**: 241–44 (Oct.).
> Running title: "On holding the breath for a lengthened period".
> Reprinted in *Experimental researches in chemistry and physics*.

See 190   On the alleged decline of science in England. By a Foreigner [G. Moll]. London, Boosey, 1833.

1834

220   Experimental researches in electricity. 6th series. 12. On the power of metals and other solids to induce the combination of gaseous bodies.

> *Phil. trans.* 1834: 55–76 (read Jan. 11).
> *See also* no. 297.

221   Experimental researches in electricity. 7th series. 11. On electro-chemical decomposition (continued). 13. On the absolute quantity of electricity associated with the particles or atoms of matter.

> *Phil. trans.* 1834: 77–122 (read Jan. 23, Feb. 6 and 13).
> *Ann. elec.* 1836–37, **1**: 305–26, 331–67.
> *Phil. mag.* 1834, **5**: 161–81, 252–64, 334–44, 424–39.
> *See also* no. 297.

3. FARADAY'S DIARY

being the record of his researches from 1820 to 1862, which he bequeathed to the Royal Institution saying in his will ". . . these I offer for the Library of the Royal Institution if the Managers should think them worth a place"

222 On the power of the platina and other solid substances to determine the combination of gaseous bodies.

> *Ath.* 1834: 90–91 (no. 327, Feb. 1).
> Unsigned abstract (by F., see *B-J* **2**: 42–44, quoting from this) of lecture at R.I. on Jan. 24.
> cf. no. 220.
> Ms. notes at R.I.

223 On the principle and action of Ericsson's caloric engine [title from ms. notes].

> *Ath.* 1834: 145 (no. 330, Feb. 22).
> *Lit. gaz.* 1834: 137 (Feb. 22).
> *Phil. mag.* 1834, **4**: 296.
> Various reports of lecture at R.I. on Feb. 14.
> Ms. notes at R.I.

224 On electro-chemical decomposition [title from ms. notes].

> *Ath.* 1834: 209 (no. 333, March 15).
> Report of lecture at R.I. on March 7.
> Ms. notes at R.I.
> cf. nos. 218 and 221.

225 On the definite action of electricity [title from ms. notes].

> *Ath.* 1834: 296 (no. 338, April 19).
> Report of lecture at R.I. on April 11.
> Ms. notes at R.I.
> cf. no. 221.

226 . . . a course of lectures on the mutual relation of electrical and chemical phenomena. May 17–June 21. Royal Institution of Great Britain, 11th April, 1834.

> Handbill. 13·5 × 10 cm.
> Syllabus of a course of six lectures at R.I. cf. *B-J* **2**: 47.
> Ms. notes at R.I.

227 Experimental researches in electricity. 8th series. 14. On the electricity of the voltaic pile; its source, quantity, intensity, and general characters.

> *Phil. trans.* 1834: 425–70 (read June 5).
> *Phil. mag.* 1835, **6**: 34–45, 125–33, 171–82, 272–79, 334–48, 410–15.
> *See also* no. 297.

228 On new applications of the products of distilled caoutchouc [title from ms. notes].

> *Lit. gaz.* 1834: 435 (June 21).
> *Lond. med. gaz.* 1833–34, **14**: 490.
> Reports of lecture at R.I. on June 13.
> Ms. notes at R.I.

[1834]

229 Letter, dated R.I. June 16, 1834, to F. O. Ward, then in his teens and a student at King's College, London.

J. Chem. Soc. 1875, **28** (n.s. **13**): 1139.
Reprinted in *Lectures delivered before the Chemical Society, Faraday lectures, 1869–1928*, 1928, p. 118.

230 On the magneto-electric spark and shock, and on a peculiar condition of electric and magneto-electric induction.

Phil. mag. 1834, **5**: 349–54 (Nov.).
Reprinted in *Experimental researches in electricity*, v. **2**.
cf. no. 231.

231 Additional observations respecting the magneto-electric spark and shock.

Phil. mag. 1834, **5**: 444–45 (Dec.).
Reprinted in *Experimental researches in electricity*, v. **2**.

232 Report from Select Committee on Metropolis Sewers.

Parl. pap. 1834 (584) **xv**.
F's evidence pp. 183–84. He appeared before the Committee on July 11.

1835

233 On Melloni's recent discoveries in radiant heat [title from ms. notes].

Lit. gaz. 1835: 73 (Jan. 31).
Report of lecture at R.I. on Jan. 23.
Ms. notes at R.I.

234 Experimental researches in electricity. 9th series. 15. On the influence by induction of an electric current on itself:—and on the inductive action of electric currents generally.

Phil. trans. 1835: 41–56 (read Jan. 29).
Ann. elec. 1836–37, **1**: 160–62, 169–86.
See also no. 297.

235 On some peculiar cases of the induction of electric currents [title from ms. notes].

Lit. gaz. 1835: 105–6 (Feb. 14).
Records of general science, 1835, **1**: 317.
Reports of lecture at R.I. on Feb. 6.
Ms. notes at R.I.
cf. no. 234.

236 On the manufacture of pens from quills and from steel—illustrated by Morden's machinery [title from ms. notes].

Lit. gaz. 1835: 216 (April 4).
Records of general science, 1835, **1**: 397–99.
Reports of lecture at R.I. on March 27.
Ms. notes at R.I.

237 Letter to William Hocking on the pneumatic railway.

> *Mech. mag.* 1835, **23**: 71 (no. 612, May 2).
>
> Dated R.I. Feb. 3, 1835.

238 Syllabus of a course of lectures on the chemical and physical properties of the common metals. May 2–June 20. Royal Institution of Great Britain, 18th April, 1835.

> Handbill. 13·5 × 10 cm.
>
> A series of eight lectures on "iron, gold, platinum, lead, copper, zinc, mercury, tin and silver" (*B-J* **2**: 68).
>
> Ms. notes at R.I.

239 An account of the water of the well Zem Zem.

> *Roy. Soc. proc.* 1830–36, **3**: 333–34.
>
> Abstract of a paper read May 14.

240 On the use of the tympanum of the ear [title from ms. notes].

> *Records of general science*, 1835, **2**: 71–72 (with title, "On sound").
>
> Abstract of lecture at R.I. on May 15.
>
> Ms. notes at R.I.

241 Experimental researches in electricity. 10th series. 16. On an improved form of the voltaic battery. 17. Some practical results respecting the construction and use of the voltaic battery.

> *Phil. trans.* 1835: 263–74 (read June 18).
>
> *Phil. mag.* 1836, **8**: 114–28.
>
> *See also* no. 297.

242 Report of the Committee on chemical notation.

> *Brit. Assoc. rep.* 1835 (pt. 1): 207 (Aug.).
>
> F. was a member of this Committee.

243 Reply to Dr. John Davy's "Remarks on certain statements of Mr. Faraday contained in his 'Researches in electricity'."

> *Edin. new phil. j.* 1835–36, **20**: 37–42 (Oct.).
>
> *Phil. mag.* 1835, **7**: 337–42.
>
> Reprinted in *Experimental researches in electricity*, v. **2**.

244 . . . 14 morning lectures in Nov. being part of a course given with Mr. Brande to students [title from ms. notes].

> "These he gave as part of Mr. Brande's morning course for the medical students of St. George's Hospital" (*B-J* **2**: 69).
>
> Ms. title is, "Electricity 1835, 6, 7, 8", but I have found nothing to corroborate that these lectures were repeated in 1836, 1837 and 1838.
>
> Ms. notes at R.I.

245　On Tory and Whig patronage to science and literature.

> *The Times*, 1835, Dec. 8: 5d.
>
> Signed W. Faraday, but by Michael F. (*see B-J 2*: 62, and Introduction p. xx).
>
> A letter dated R.I. Dec. 7 in answer to an article from *Fraser's Magazine*, Dec. 1835, which purported to give an account of a conversation between F. and Lord Melbourne on a proposed pension for F. This article was reprinted in *The Times* of Nov. 28. *See B-J 2*: 56–64, 116–123.

See 395a Letter on action of seawater on cast iron and bronze, dated R.I. 28 Dec. 1835.

246　A course of elementary lectures on electricity.

> Christmas juvenile lectures, 1835, Dec. 29 to 1836, Jan. 9. See *B-J 2*: 69.
>
> Ms. notes at R.I.

247　Report from the Committee appointed to investigate Mr. Kyan's patent for the prevention of dry rot.

> *Parl. pap.* 1835 (367) xlviii.
>
> F's evidence, given on May 4, 1835, pp. 13–14; letters from F. dated May 29 and June 1, 1835, pp. 23–24. cf. no. 210.

1836

248　Silicified plants and fossils [title from ms. notes].

> *Lit. gaz.* 1836: 72 (Jan. 30).
> *Lond. med. gaz.* 1835–36, **17**: 693.
> *Records of general science*, 1836, **3**: 155–56.
>
> Reports of lecture at R.I. on Jan. 22.
> Ms. notes at R.I.

249　On magnetism of metals as a general property [title from ms. notes].

> *Lit. gaz.* 1836: 137 (Feb. 27).
> *Lond. med. gaz.* 1835–36, **17**: 909–11.
>
> Reports of a lecture at R.I. on Feb. 19.
> Ms. notes at R.I.
> cf. no. 250.

250　On the general magnetic relations and characters of the metals.

> *Phil. mag.* 1836, **8**: 177–81 (March).
>
> Reprinted in *Experimental researches in electricity*, v. **2**.
> *See also* no. 293.

251　Syllabus of a course of lectures on the philosophy of heat . . . April 16th–May 21st. Royal Institution of Great Britain, 12th April 1836.

> Handbill. 13·5 × 10 cm.
> Six lectures.
> Ms. notes at R.I.

252 On plumbago and pencils.
>   *Lond. med. gaz.* 1835–36, **18**: 267.
>   *Records of general science,* 1836, **3**: 468–69.
>   Report of lecture at R.I. on April 29.
>   Ms. notes at R.I.

253 Considerations respecting chemical elements [title from ms. notes].
>   *Lond. med. gaz.* 1835–36, **18**: 462, with title, "On the probable ultimate analysis of chemical substances".
>   Report of lecture at R.I. on June 10.
>   Ms. notes at R.I.

254 On a supposed new sulphate and oxide of antimony.
>   *Phil. mag.* 1836, **8**: 476–79 (June).
>   Reprinted in *Experimental researches in electricity,* v. **2**.

255 On the history of the condensation of the gases, in reply to Dr. Davy, introduced by some remarks on that of electro-magnetic rotation.
>   *Phil. mag.* 1836, **8**: 521–29 (June).
>   Reprinted in *Experimental researches in ehemistry and physics,* and in *Experimental researches in electricity,* v. **2**.

256 Notice of the magnetic action of manganese at low temperatures, as stated by M. Berthier. In a letter from Mr. Faraday.
>   *Phil. mag.* 1836, **9**: 65–66 (July).
>   Reprinted in *Experimental researches in electricity,* v. **2**.

257 On a peculiar voltaic condition of iron, by Prof. Schoenbein, of Bâle; in a letter to Mr. Faraday: with further experiments on the same subject, by Mr. Faraday.
>   *Phil. mag.* 1836, **9**: 53–65 (July).
>   Reprinted in *Experimental researches in electricity,* v. **2**.

258 Letter from Mr. Faraday to Mr. Brayley on some former researches relative to the peculiar voltaic condition of iron reobserved by Prof. Schoenbein.
>   *Phil. mag.* 1836, **9**: 122–23 (Aug.).
>   Reprinted in *Experimental researches in electricity,* v. **2**.

259 Aurora borealis observed in the Isle of Wight, on August 10th [1836].
>   *Phil. mag.* 1836, **9**: 230 (Sept.).
>   Signed M.F. and noted in F's copy of *Experimental researches in chemistry and physics* at I.E.E. (*see* Introduction, p. xv).

See 210 On the practical prevention of dry rot. London, J. Weale, 1836.

260   On Mossotti's reference of electrical attraction, the attraction of aggregation, and the attraction of gravitation to one cause.

> *Ath.* 1837: 67 (no. 483, Jan. 28).
> *Lit. gaz.* 1837: 72 (Feb. 4).
> *Phil. mag.* 1837, **10**: 317–18.
> Various reports of lecture at R.I. on Jan 20.
> Ms. notes at R.I.

261   On Dr. Marshall Hall's reflex function of the spinal marrow.

> *Lit. gaz.* 1837: 126–27 (Feb. 25).
> *Lond. med. gaz.* 1836–37, **19**: 828–29.
> Reports of lecture at R.I. on Feb. 17.

262   On Mr. Cowper's parlour printing press.

> *Phil. mag.* 1837, **10**: 318, giving both Marshall Hall and printing press as lectures (titles only) by F. at R.I. on Feb. 17.

263   Correction [a letter correcting "erroneous statement which has appeared in several journals" that F. had confirmed the results of Mr. Crosse, "who states he has obtained living insects by agency of electricity and silica"].

> *Lit. gaz.* 1837: 147 (no. 1050, March 4).
> Letter dated R.I. March 2.
> *The Times*, 1837, March 4: 6b.
> Letter dated R.I. March 3.

264   On De la Rue's mode of applying sulphate of copper to the exaltation of the powers of a common voltaic battery.

> *Lond. med. gaz.* 1836–37, **19**: 968–69.
> Report of lecture at R.I. on March 17.

265   Remarks on Faraday's hypothesis with regard to the causes of the neutrality of iron in nitric acid. By Prof. Schoenbein [and] Note from Prof. Faraday to Mr. Richard Taylor on the preceding paper.

> *Phil. mag.* 1837, **10**: 172–76 (March).
> F's Note, pp. 175–76.

266   Syllabus of a course of six lectures on the ancient elements, earth, air, fire, water. April 8th–May 13th, Royal Institution of Great Britain, 25th March, 1837.

> Handbill. 22·5 × 18·5 cm.
> Ms. notes at R.I.

4. THE FRONT OF THE ROYAL INSTITUTION ABOUT 1840
(from a contemporary watercolour by T. Hosmer Shepherd)

Faraday delivering one of his Christmas Juvenile Lectures in 1856 with the Prince Consort in the
Chair accompanied by the young Prince Albert (later Edward VII) and his brother

267 On a peculiar condition of iron in relation to its chemical affinity and its electromotive force.

> *Lit. gaz.* 1837: 289 (May 6).
> *Lond. med. gaz.* 1836–37, **20**: 197–98.
> Reports of lecture at R.I. on April 28.
> Ms. notes at R.I.

268 On the early arts.

> *Lit. gaz.* 1837: 384–85 (June 17).
> *Lond. med. gaz.* 1836–37, **20**: 441, with title, "On the cutting instruments and arrows of savage nations".
> Reports of lecture at R.I. on June 9.
> Ms. notes at R.I.

269 On Mr. Cocking's death from a parachute descent.

> *The Times*, 1837, Aug. 1: 5d.
> Letter dated R.I. July 31.
> Reprinted in *Mech. mag.* 1837, **27**: 302 (no. 730, Aug. 5); report of inquest on Cocking appears *ibid.* pp. 297–302.

270 Letter to William Jerdan, editor of *Literary gazette*, correcting statement that knighthood conferred on F.

> *Trans. Rochdale Lit. Sci. Soc.* 1929–31, **17**: front.
> Letter, dated R.I. Aug. 15, 1837, was shown at a meeting of the Society on Dec. 14, 1928. It was lent to the Society by Mrs. Charles A. Faraday of Birmingham.
> cf. *Nature*, 1931, **128**: 697.

271 On a communication from Dr. Apjohn on a new variety of alum at the British Association meeting, 1837, Sept. 13, Sheffield.

> *Ath.* 1837: 694 (no. 517, Sept. 23).
> A report of a discussion.

272 On Prof. Graham's paper on inorganic salts at the British Association meeting, 1837, Sept. 13, Sheffield.

> *Ath.* 1837: 695 (no. 517, Sept. 23) } the same.
> *Phil. mag.* 1837, **11**: 398.
> A report of a discussion.

273 Experimental researches in electricity. 11th series. 18. On induction.

> *Phil. trans.* 1838: 1–40 (read 1837, Dec. 21).
> *Ann. elec.* 1839–40, **4**: 1–25, 81–104.
> *Phil. mag.* 1838, **13**: 281–99, 355–67, 412–30.
> *See also* nos. 277, 279, 280 and 297.

274 A course of six elementary lectures on chemistry adapted to a juvenile auditory, 1837, Dec. 28 to 1838, Jan. 9.

> Ms. notes at R.I. The same notes as for the Christmas lectures of 1827–28, *see* no. 151.

See 210   On the practical prevention of dry rot. London, J. Weale, 1837.

1838

275   On electrical induction.

> *Lond. med. gaz.* 1837–38, **1**: 703–4.
> Report of lecture at R.I. on Jan. 19.
> Short (verbatim) extract, "On the folly of sprinkling salt upon snow", in *The Times*, 1838, Jan. 22: 7c. (?)
> Ms. notes at R.I.

276   On the nature of fatty bodies, and on the application of stearine to the manufacture of candles.

> *Lond. med. gaz.* 1837–38, **1**: 748–49.
> Report of lecture at R.I. on Jan. 26.

277   Experimental researches in electricity. 12th series. 18. On induction, continued.

> *Phil. trans.* 1838: 83–123 (read Feb. 8).
> *Ann. elec.* 1840, **5**: 81–104, 161–86.
> *See also* nos. 273, 279 and 297.

278   On the atmosphere of this and other planets.

> *Lit. gaz.* 1838: 137 (March 3).
> *Lond. med. gaz.* 1837–38, **1**: 910.
> Reports of lecture at R.I. on Feb. 2.
> Ms. notes at R.I.

279   Experimental researches in electricity. 13th series. 18. On induction, continued. 19. Nature of the electric current.

> *Phil. trans.* 1838: 125–68 (read March 15).
> *Ann. elec.* 1840, **5**: 255–84, 321–36.
> *See also* nos. 273, 277 and 297.

280   Supplementary note to Experimental researches in electricity. 11th series.

> *Phil. trans.* 1838: 79–81 (received March 29).
> *Ann. elec.* 1839–40, **4**: 229–31.
> *See also* nos. 273 and 297.

281   On Mr. Ward's method of preserving plants in limited atmospheres.

> *Lit. gaz.* 1838: 233 (April 14).
> Report of lecture at R.I. on April 6.
> Ms. notes at R.I.

282   Eight lectures on electricity, April 28 to June 16.

> Noted in *B-J* **2**: 87.
> Ms. notes at R.I.

283 On the solid, liquid, and gaseous state of carbonic acid, illustrated by Thilorier's apparatus.

> *Lit. gaz.* 1838: 326–27 (May 26).
> Report of lecture at R.I. on May 18.
> Ms. notes at R.I.

284 On the relation of insulation and conduction of electricity.

> *Lit. gaz.* 1838: 378 (June 16).
> Short report of lecture at R.I. on June 8.
> cf. no. 285.
> Ms. notes at R.I.

285 Experimental researches in electricity. 14th series. 20. Nature of the electric force or forces. 21. Relation of the electric and magnetic forces. 22. Note on electrical excitation.

> *Phil. trans.* 1838: 265–82 (read June 21).
> *Ann. elec.* 1840, **5**: 407–26.
> *See also* no. 297.

286 Experimental researches in electricity. 15th series. 23. Notice of the character and direction of the electric force of the Gymnotus.

> *Phil. trans.* 1839: 1–12 (read 1838, Dec. 6).
> *Phil. mag.* 1839, **15**: 358–72.
> *See also* no. 297.

1839

287 On the Gymnotus and torpedo.

> *Lit. gaz.* 1839: 57–58 (Jan. 26).
> Report of lecture at R.I. on Jan. 18.
> cf. no. 286.
> Ms. notes at R.I.

288 Remarks on corrosion.

> *Min. proc. Instn. Civ. Engrs.* 1839, **1**: 34.
> Abstract of a discussion at a meeting of the Institution on Feb. 5.

289 Remarks on resin fuel.

> *Min. proc. Instn. Civ. Engrs.* 1839, **1**: 35–36.
> Abstract of a discussion at a meeting of the Institution on Feb. 5.

290 On Gurney's oxy-oil, or Bude lamp for lighthouses and other situations.

> *Ath.* 1839: 157–58 (no. 591).
> *Lit. gaz.* 1839: 121–22 (Feb. 23).
> *The Times* 1839, Feb. 19: 6b.
> Various reports of lecture at R.I. on Feb. 15.
> Ms. notes at R.I.

291　Chemical account of the Cold Bokkeveld meteoric stone, in a letter addressed to Sir J. F. W. Herschel.

> *Phil. trans.* 1839: 86–87 (read March 21).

292　On Prof. Airy's method of correcting the compass in iron vessels.

> *Lit. gaz.* 1839: 201 (March 30).
> *Mech. mag.* 1839, **31**: 29–30 (no. 818, April 13).
> Reports of lecture at R.I. on March 22.
> Ms. notes at R.I.

293　On the general magnetic relations and characters of the metals; additional facts.

> *Phil. mag.* 1839, **14**: 161–63 (March).
> Reprinted in *Experimental researches in electricity*, v. **2**.
> *See also* no. 250.

294　Eight lectures on the chemistry of the non-metallic elements: oxygen, chlorine, hydrogen, nitrogen, phosphorus, sulphur, carbon [title from ms. notes].

> A course of lectures at the R.I., April 13 to June 1. *See B-J* **2**: 103–4.
> Ms. notes at R.I.

295　Some general remarks on flame [title from ms. notes].

> *Mech. mag.* 1839, **31**: 126 (no. 824, May 25).
> Report of lecture at R.I. on May 10.
> Ms. notes at R.I.

296　On Hullmandel's mode of producing designs and patterns on metallic surfaces.

> *Lit. gaz.* 1839: 377 (June 15).
> *The Times* 1839, June 7: 5b.
> Reports of lecture at R.I. on June 7.
> Ms. notes at R.I.

297　Experimental researches in electricity. Reprinted from the *Philosophical transactions* of 1831–1852. With other electrical papers from the *Quarterly journal of science, Philosophical magazine* [and] the *Proceedings of the Royal Institution*. London, Taylor and Francis, 1839–55.

> 3 v. diagrs. fold. plates. 23 cm.
> V. 2 was published in 1844.
> "The readers of the volume will, I hope, do me the justice to remember that it was not written as a *whole*, but in parts; the earlier portions rarely having any known relation at the time to those which might follow." (From Preface to v. 1.)
> Reviewed in *Phil. mag.* 1839, **14**: 468–72; *Phil. mag.* 1855, **10**: 295–99; *Westminster review*, 1856, **9**: 254–60.

1849

Experimental researches in electricity. Reprinted from the *Philosophical transactions* of 1831–1838. V. 1. 2nd ed. London, R. and J. E. Taylor, 1849.

> Copy (not seen) at Institution of Civil Engineers, London.

1878–1882?

Experimental researches in electricity . . . 3 v. London, Bernard Quaritch, 1839–55. Facsimile reprint [1878–82?].

> Quaritch had purchased the copyright from Mrs. Faraday, together with the remaining stocks of v. 3, and with her permission issued this facsimile reprint of v. 1–2. Taylor and Francis, the original printers, executed the reprint. *See* letter from Quaritch, *Nature*, 1878, **17**: 342, together with letters of complaint from S. P. Thompson, *ibid.*, pp. 304 and 361. V. 3 reprinted 1882? (*English catalogue.*)

1912

Experimental researches in electricity. London, J. M. Dent [1912].

> xxii, 336 pp. diagr. 17·5 cm. (Everyman's library).
>
> In the 1922 reprint, date of first printing is wrongly given as 1914.
>
> "The present select edition . . . consists of series 3–8 and 16, 17 of the original issue in three volumes, 1839–55, with the plates and figures distributed for the reader's convenience in the text, and the sections and paragraphs consecutively renumbered." (p. xix.)
>
> The introduction is by John Tyndall and comprises the Summary and concluding passages of his *Faraday as a discoverer*. 1868.
>
> This Everyman's ed. was subsequently reprinted in 1922, 1931, 1938, 1940, 1943 and 1951.
>
> *Note:* For bound collection of offprints from *Phil. trans. see* no. 427.

1840

298   On voltaic precipitations—electrotype [title from ms. notes].

> *Lit. gaz.* 1840: 74 (Feb. 1).
> Report of lecture at R.I. on Jan. 24.
> Ms. notes at R.I.

299   Experimental researches in electricity. 16th and 17th series. 24. On the source of power in the voltaic pile.

> *Phil. trans.* 1840: 61–91, 93–127 (read Feb. 6 and March 19).
> *Phil. mag.* 1843, **22**: 477–80 reprints paras. 2065–73 with title, "On the chemical and contact theories of the voltaic battery".
> *See also* no. 297.

300   On a particular relation, Dove's, of condensable gases and steam.

> *Phil. mag.* 1840, **16**: 338.
> Title (only) of lecture at R.I. on Feb. 7.
> Ms. notes at R.I.

301   A course of seven lectures on chemistry, May 2 to June 13, at R.I.

> *B-J* **2**: 104 "he gave seven lectures on the force usually called chemical affinity".
> Ms. notes at R.I.

302 On the origin of electricity in the voltaic pile.
> *Phil. mag.* 1840, **17**: 74.
> Title (only) of lecture at R.I. on May 8.
> Ms. notes at R.I.
> cf. no. 299.

303 An answer to Dr. Hare's letter on certain theoretical opinions [on static induction].
> *Phil. mag.* 1840, **17**: 54–65 (July).
> *Ann. elec.* 1840, **5**: 110–20.
> Reprinted in *Experimental researches in electricity*, v. **2**.

304 On magneto-electric induction in a letter to M. Gay-Lussac.
> *Phil. mag.* 1840, **17**: 281–89, 356–66 (Oct.–Nov.).

305 On the electricity of a jet of steam issuing from a boiler. By H. G. Armstrong, in letters to Prof. Faraday.
> *Phil. mag.* 1840, **17**: 370–74 (Nov.).
> A short note by F. is appended to this article.

1841

306 On some supposed forms of lightning.
> *Phil. mag.* 1841, **19**: 104–6 (Aug.).
> *Ann. elec.* 1841, **7**: 228–30.
> Reprinted in *Experimental researches in electricity*, v. **2**.

307 . . . A course of six lectures on the rudiments of chemistry adapted to a juvenile auditory. Dec. 28th, 1841–Jan. 8th. Royal Institution of Great Britain, 6th December, 1841.
> Handbill. 13·5 × 10 cm.
> Prospectus for the Christmas lectures at R.I.
> Ms. notes at R.I.

1842

308 Observations on the composition of pig-iron.
> *Min. proc. Instn. Civ. Engrs.* 1842, **2**: 61.
> Abstract of discussion at a meeting of the Institution on Feb. 8.

309 On conduction in lightning rods.
> *Lit. gaz.* 1842: 279 (April 23).
> Report of lecture at R.I. on April 15.
> Ms. notes at R.I.

310 On Hullmandel's process [of lithography and lithotinting].

        Lit. gaz. 1842: 424 (June 18).

        Report of lecture at R.I. on June 10.

        Ms. notes at R.I.

See 153 Chemical manipulation. 3rd ed. 1842.

1843

311 Radial images.

        Lit. gaz. 1843: 7 (no. 1355, Jan. 7).

        Letter to editor of *Lit. gaz.* dated R.I. Jan. 5.

312 On some phenomena of electric induction.

        Rep. pat. invent. 1843, **1**: 165–84.

        Lecture at R.I. on Jan. 20.

        Reports in: *Chem. gaz.* 1842–43, **1**: 194–95; *Lit. gaz.* 1843: 55–56 (Jan. 28).

        Ms. notes at R.I.

313 Experimental researches in electricity. 18th series. 25. On the electricity evolved by the friction of water and steam against other bodies.

        Phil. trans. 1843: 17–32 (read Feb. 2).

        See also no. 297.

314 On Clay's process of iron-making.

        Min. proc. Instn. Civ. Engrs. 1843, **2**: 86.

        Abstract of discussion at meeting of the Institution on Feb. 14.

315 On static electrical inductive action.

        Phil. mag. 1843, **22**: 200–4 (March).

        Reprinted in *Experimental researches in electricity,* v. **2**.

316 On light and ventilation.

        Rep. pat. invent. 1843, **2**: 174–81, 238–50.

        Lecture at R.I. on April 7.

        Reports in: *Ath.* 1843: 394 (no. 808, April 22); *Lit. gaz.* 1843: 259–60 (April 22).

        Ms. notes at R.I.

317 Eight lectures at R.I. on electricity, April 29–June 17.

        Ms. notes at R.I.

        See *B-J* **2**: 161.

318 On Dr. Hare's second letter, and on the chemical and contact theories of the voltaic battery.

        Phil. mag. 1843, **22**: 268–69 (April).

        Reprinted in *Experimental researches in electricity,* v. **2**.

319 Electricity of steam.

> *Rep. pat. invent.* 1843, **2**: 49–55, 114–22.
> Lecture at R.I. on June 9.
> Reports in: *Chem. gaz.* 1842–43, **1**: 443–44; *Phil. mag.* 1843, **22**: 570; *Lit. gaz.* 1843: 416 (June 24).
> Ms. notes at R.I.

320 On the ventilation of lamp burners.

> *Min. proc. Instn. Civ. Engrs.* 1843, **2**: 188–90.
> Abstract of discussion at meeting of Institution on June 13, after paper by James Faraday (F's nephew).

321 On the ventilation of lighthouse lamps; the points necessary to be observed, and the manner in which these have been or may be attained.

> *Min. proc. Instn. Civ. Engrs.* 1843, **2**: 206–9.
> Abstract (by F.) of lecture at the Institution on June 27.
> Reprinted in *Experimental researches in chemistry and physics.*

See 299   On the chemical and contact theories of the voltaic battery.

> *Phil. mag.* 1843, **22**: 477–80 (June).

See 344   Report on lightning rods of lighthouses, dated 25th Sept., 1843.

322 Letter to Lieut. Manley Dixon giving an analysis of seawater. (*In: An account of a remarkably large and luminous spot in the sea.* By Captain F. Eardley Wilmot.)

> *Roy. Soc. proc.* 1843–50, **5**: 476 (read Nov. 23).
> Letter dated R.I. Sept. 25, 1843.

323 . . . A course of six lectures on the first principles of electricity adapted to a juvenile auditory. 26th December–6th January, 1844. Royal Institution of Great Britain, 11th December, 1843.

> Handbill. 13×9·5 cm.
> Syllabus of the Christmas lectures at R.I.
> Ms. notes at R.I.

1844

324 A speculation touching electric conduction and the nature of matter.

> *Ath.* 1844: 90 (no. 848, Jan. 27).
> *Chem. gaz.* 1844, **2**: 81–82.
> *Lit. gaz.* 1844: 60–61 (Jan. 27).
> Various reports of lecture at R.I. on Jan. 19.
> cf. no. 325.

325 A speculation touching electric conduction and the nature of matter.

    Phil. mag. 1844, **24**: 136–44 (Feb.).

    Elaboration of a lecture at R.I., cf. no. 324.

    Reprinted in *Experimental researches in electricity*, v. **2**.

326 On the philosophy and phenomena of heat.

    Civil eng. 1844, **7**: 234–36, 288–89, 318–19, 358, 385.

    Reports of a course of 8 lectures at R.I., April 20–June 8.

    Ms. notes at R.I.

327 On recent improvements in the manufacture and silvering of mirrors.

    Ath. 1844: 554–55 (no. 868, June 15) ⎱

    Chem. gaz. 1844, **2**: 315–16   ⎰ the same.

    Civil eng. 1844, **7**: 248–49 (June).

    Lit. gaz. 1844: 384 (June 15).

    Various reports of lecture at R.I. (*Civ. eng.* says at R.I.B.A.) on June 7.

    Ms. notes at R.I.

See 343 Letter to Sir Byam Martin, respecting the action of seawater on iron.

    Dated R.I. June 12, 1844.

See 297 Experimental researches in electricity. V. 2. London, 1844.

1845

328 On the liquefaction and solidification of bodies generally existing as gases.

    Phil. trans. 1845: 155–77 (read Jan. 9 and Feb. 20).

    Reprinted in *Experimental researches in chemistry and physics*, and in *The liquefaction of gases* (Alembic Club reprint no. 12) (nos. 458 and 483).

    See also no. 333.

329 The ventilation of mines, and the means of preventing explosions from fire damp.

    Civ. eng. 1845, **8**: 115–118 (no. 91, April).

    Rep. pat. invent. 1845, **5**: 191–211.

    Lecture at R.I. on Jan. 17.

    Ms. notes at R.I.

    cf. no. 335.

330 On the liquefaction and solidification of gases.

    Civ. eng. 1845, **8**: 87–88 (no. 90 March).

    Lit. gaz. 1845: 89 (no. 1464, Feb. 8).

    The Times 1845, Feb. 4: 4f.

    Various reports of lecture at R.I. on Jan. 31.

    Ms. notes at R.I.

    cf. no. 328.

331   Lettre à M. Dumas sur la liquéfaction des gaz.

> *Ann. chim.* 1845, **13**: 120–24 (Jan.).
>
> *Bibl. univ.* 1844, **54**: 189–92 (1844, Nov., with note that reprinted from *Ann. chim.* Evidently an antedated issue, cf. no. 334).
>
> An English translation appears in *Chem. gaz.* 1845, **3**: 56–58; *Civ. eng.* 1845, **8**: 87–88 (no. 90, March).

332   Report from Messrs. Faraday and Lyell to the Rt. Hon. Sir James Graham, Bart., Secretary of State for the Home Department, on the subject of the explosion at the Haswell Collieries, and on the means of preventing similar accidents.

> *Phil. mag.* 1845, **26**: 16–35 (Jan.).
>
> *Parl. pap.* 1845 (232) xvi, which also contains the "Report addressed to the United Committee of the Coal Trade . . . ; and the Reply of Messrs. Lyell and Faraday thereto".

333   Additional remarks respecting the condensation of gases.

> *Roy. Soc. proc.* 1843–50, **5**: 547 (read Feb. 20).
>
> Reprinted in *Experimental researches in chemistry and physics.*
>
> *See also* no. 328.

334   Sur la liquéfaction et la solidification des gaz. Extrait d'une lettre à M. le prof. de la Rive.

> *Bibl. univ.* 1844, **53**: 390 (an antedated issue).
>
> A letter of Feb. 20, 1845, cf. *B-J* **2**: 186–88.

335   On the ventilation of the coal mine goaf.

> *Phil. mag.* 1845, **26**: 169–70 (Feb.).
>
> Includes account of "some practical results which were brought generally before our members here at the last Friday Evening Meeting". cf. no. 329.

336   Eight lectures at Royal Institution on certain metals and metallic properties, April 12 to May 31.

> *Lond. med. gaz.* 1845, **1**: 47–52, 132–37, 397–402, 1274–78, 1363–68; 1846, **2**: 360–64, 579–84, 711–16.
>
> Ms. notes at R.I.

337   Anastatic printing.

> *Ath.* 1845: 437 (no. 914, May 3).
>
> *Lit. gaz.* 1845: 279 (no. 1476, May 3).
>
> Reports of lecture at R.I. on April 25.
>
> Ms. notes at R.I.

338   On artesian wells and water.

> *Ath.* 1845, 568–69 (no. 919, June 7).
>
> *Lit. gaz.* 1845: 361 (no. 1481, June 7).
>
> Reports of lecture at R.I. on May 30.
>
> Ms. notes at R.I.

339 Remarks on mining accidents.

    Ath. 1845: 746 (no. 926, July 26).

    Report of comment by F. at meeting of Section C of the British Association on June 19 (?). B.A. meeting was from June 19–23.

340 On the magnetic relations and characters of the metals.

    Phil. mag. 1845, **27**: 1–3 (July).

    Reprinted in *Experimental researches in electricity*, v. **2**.

341 Experimental researches in electricity. 19th–21st series. 26. On the magnetization of light and the illumination of magnetic lines of force. 27. On new magnetic actions, and on the magnetic condition of all matter.

    Phil. trans. 1846: 1–62 (19th series read Nov. 20; 20th series read Dec. 18; 21st series read 1846, Jan. 8).

    Phil. mag. 1846, 28: 294–317 (19th series), 396–468 (20th series).

    Reviewed in *Quarterly review* 1846, **79**: 93–126.

    See also no. 297.

342 Extrait d'une lettre à M. de la Rive [dated Brighton, Dec. 4, 1845].

    Bibl. univ. Arch. 1846, **1**: 72–76 (Jan. ?).

    Given in English in *B-J*, **2**: 206–9.

343 Syllabus of a course of six lectures on the rudiments of chemistry adapted to a juvenile auditory . . . 27th December–8th January. Royal Institution of Great Britain, 17th November, 1845.

    Handbill. 13·5 × 10 cm.

    Ms. notes at R.I.

344 Letter to Sir Byam Martin, respecting the action of seawater on iron. (*In: Report of the Commissioners on Harbours of Refuge, 1845.* Appendix A, p. 198.)

    Dated R.I. 1844, June 12.

    Parl. pap. 1845 [611] xvi.

    Mech. mag. 1845, **43**: 89–90 (no. 1148, Aug. 9).

    Signed W. Faraday in both. (*See* Introduction p. xx.)

See 332 Report of Messrs. Lyell and Faraday to the Secretary of State for the Home Department, on the . . . explosion at the Haswell Collieries in September last:—Also, Report addressed to the United Committee of the Coal Trade . . . ; and the Reply of Messrs. Lyell and Faraday thereto.

345 Report on the lightning rods of lighthouses. (*In: Report from the Select Committee on lighthouses,* pp. 480–81.)

    Parl. pap. 1845 (607) ix.

    Reprinted in *Lightning Rod Conference (1878–1881).* Edited by G. J. Symons. London, 1882, pp. 183–86, where dated 25th Sept., 1843.

346 Sur de nouvelles relations entre l'électricité, la lumière et le magnétisme. Extrait d'une lettre de M. Faraday à M. Dumas.

> *Comptes rendus de l'Acad. Sci.* 1846, **22**: 113–15.
> *Bibl. univ. Arch.* 1846, **1**: 77–79.
> Communicated to the Academy on Jan. 19.
> Extracts in English in *Lit. gaz.* 1846: 109 (Jan. 31).

347 Magnetization of light [title from ms. notes].

> *Ath.* 1846: 126 (no. 953, Jan. 31).
> Report of lecture at R.I. on Jan. 23.
> Ms. notes at R.I.
> cf. no. 341.

348 Rust.

> *Mech. mag.* 1846, **44**: 160 (no. 1176, Feb. 21).
> *Yrbk. facts*, 1847: 183–84.
> Extract from ?

349 On the magnetic condition of matter.

> *Lit. gaz.* 1846: 265–66 (March 21).
> Report of lecture at R.I. on March 6.

350 On Wheatstone's electro-magnetic chronoscope.

> *Ath.* 1846: 429 (no. 965, April 25).
> *Lit. gaz.* 1846: 340–41 (April 11).
> Reports of lecture at R.I. on April 3.
> Ms. notes at R.I.

351 A course of lectures on electricity and magnetism.

> *Lond. med. gaz.* 1846, **2**: 977–82; 1846, **3**: 1–7, 89–95, 177–82, 265–71, 353–58, 441–47, 523–29.
> 8 lectures at R.I. April 25–June 13.

352 On the quality of lime preserved for fresco painting.

> *Civ. eng.* 1846, **9**: 117 (no. 103, April).

353 Thoughts on ray-vibrations.

> *Phil. mag.* 1846, **28**: 345–50 (May).
> Reprinted in *Experimental researches in chemistry and physics*, and in *Experimental researches in electricity*, v. **3**.

354 On the cohesive force of water.

> *Lit. gaz.* 1846: 560 (June 20).
> *Lond. med. gaz.* 1846, **2**: 1096–98.
> Reports of lecture at R.I. on June 12.
> Ms. notes at R.I.

355   On the magnetic affection of light, and on the distinction between the ferromagnetic and diamagnetic conditions of matter.

> *Phil. mag.* 1846, **29**: 153–56, 249–58 (Sept. and Oct.).
> Reprinted in *Experimental researches in electricity*, v. **3**.

1847

356   On gunpowder.

> *Ath.* 1847: 128–29 (no. 1005, Jan. 30).
> *Lond. med. gaz.* 1847, **4**: 198–201.
> Reports of lecture at R.I. on Jan. 22.
> Ms. notes at R.I.

357   On Mr. Barry's plan of ventilating the House of Lords.

> *Ath.* 1847: 366–67 (no. 1014, April 3).
> *Lit. gaz.* 1847: 263–64 (April 3).
> Reports of lecture at R.I. on March 26.
> Ms. notes at R.I.

358   Congélation du mercure en trois secondes, en vertu de l'état sphéroïdal, dans un creuset incandescent. Extrait d'une lettre de M. Faraday à M. Boutigny d'Évreux.

> *Ann. chim.* 1847, **19**: 383 (March).
> English translation in *American journal of science* (Silliman), 1847, **4**: 101.

359   Eight lectures on physics and chemical philosophy, April 17–June 12.

> cf. *B-J* **2**: 223–25.
> Ms. notes at R.I.

360   On the steam-jet.

> *Ath.* 1847: 648–49 (no. 1025, June 19).
> *Lit. gaz.* 1847: 447 (June 19).
> Reports of lecture at R.I. on June 11.
> Ms. notes at R.I.

361   On certain specimens of diamond subjected to intense heat.

> *Brit. Assoc. rep.* 1847 (pt. 2): 50 (June 23–30).
> Report of remarks by F. on an experiment by Jacquelin.

362   Discourse on the magnetic condition of matter, delivered in the Theatre on Friday evening, June 25.

> *Brit. Assoc. rep.* 1847 (pt. 2): 20–21.
> A report.

363   On the diamagnetic conditions of flame and gases.

> *Phil. mag.* 1847, **31**: 401–21 (Dec.)
> Reprinted in *Experimental researches in electricity*, v. **3**.

364 Letter to C. R. Weld denying that F. knighted. Dated R.I. 1848, Jan. 8.

J. chem. ed. 1949, **26**: 441–42.

Facsimile and transcription of the letter, which is now in the Library of the American Philosophical Society, Philadelphia.

365 Remarks on the manufacture of artificial stone with a silica base.

Min. proc. Instn. Civ. Engrs. 1848, **7**: 60–65.

Abstract of discussion at a meeting of the Institution on Jan. 11.

366 On the use of gutta percha in electrical insulation.

Phil. mag. 1848, **32**: 165–67 (March).
Edin. new phil. j. 1847–48, **44**: 295–97.

Reprinted in *Experimental researches in electricity*, v. **3**.

367 The diamagnetic condition of flame.

Ath. 1848: 417 (no. 1069, April 22).
Civ. eng. 1848, **11**: 187 (no. 129, June).
Lit. gaz. 1848: 280 (April 22).

Various reports of lecture at R.I. on April 14.
Ms. notes at R.I.

368 On the allied phenomena of the chemical and electrical forces.

Civ. eng. 1848, **11**: 219–21 (no. 130, July).

Report of a course of 7 lectures at the R.I., May 6–June 17.
Ms. notes at R.I.

369 Two recent inventions of artificial stone.

Ath. 1848: 607 (no. 1077, June 17).
Lit. gaz. 1848: 376–77 (June 3).

Reports of lecture at R.I. on May 26.
Ms. notes at R.I.

370 On the conversion of diamond into coke by the electric flame.

Ath. 1848: 682 (no. 1080, July 8).
Lit. gaz. 1848: 424–25 (June 24).

Reports of lecture at R.I. on June 16.
Ms. notes at R.I.

371 Experimental researches in electricity. 22nd series. 28. On the crystalline polarity of bismuth and other bodies, and on its relation to the magnetic form of force.

Phil. trans. 1849: 1–41 (read 1848, Dec. 7).

See also no. 297.

372 Syllabus of a course of six lectures on the chemical history of a candle, intended for a juvenile auditory. 28th December, 1848–9th [January]. Royal Institution of Great Britain, December 1860 [sic].

> Handbill. 14 × 10 cm.
>
> Ms. notes at R.I.; their title indicates F. used same notes for Christmas lectures 1854–55 and 1860–61.
>
> *See* nos. 419 and 464.

1849

373 On the crystalline polarity of bismuth and other bodies, and on its relation to the magnetic force.

> *Lit. gaz.* 1849: 96–97 (no. 1673, Feb. 10).
> *Lond. med. gaz.* 1849, **8**: 212–13.
> Reports of lecture at R.I. on Jan. 26 (?) (*Lit. gaz.* says Jan. 19), cf. *B-J* **2**: 238.
> Ms. notes at R.I. for lecture on magnecrystallic phenomena on Jan. 26.
> cf. no. 371.

374 On magnetic and diamagnetic bodies.

> A private lecture to Prince Albert at R.I. on Feb. 26, cf. *B-J* **2**: 238–39.
> Ms. notes at R.I.

375 On Plücker's repulsion of the optic axes of crystals by the magnetic poles.

> *Ath.* 1849: 360 (no. 1119, April 7).
> *Lit. gaz.* 1849: 259 (no. 1681, April 7).
> *Lond. med. gaz.* 1849, **8**: 741–42.
> Various reports of lecture at R.I. on March 30.
> Ms. notes at R.I.

376 Eight lectures on static electricity.

> A course of lectures at the R.I. after Easter (April 21?→), cf. *B-J* **2**: 237–38.
> Ms. notes at R.I.

377 On envelope machinery.

> *Ath.* 1849: 601 (no. 1128, June 9).
> *Lit. gaz.* 1849: 431 (no. 1690, June 9).
> Reports of lecture at R.I. on June 1.
> Ms. notes at R.I.

378 The power of Mr. Gassiot's battery in exciting light and heat.

> *Birmingham journal*, 1849, **25**: 7 (no. 1270, Sept. 15).
> Report of talk at British Association meeting on Sept. 13.

See 297 Experimental researches in electricity, v. 1. 2nd ed. 1849.

379   Remarks on the chemical changes which water undergoes in passing through chalk.

> *Min. proc. Instn. Civ. Engrs.* 1849–50, **9**: 160–61.
> Abstract of discussion at meeting of the Institution on Jan. 22.

380   On the electricity of the air.

> *Ath.* 1850: 161–62 (no. 1163, Feb. 9).
> *Lit. gaz.* 1850: 108 (Feb. 9).
> Reports of lecture at R.I. on Feb. 1.
> Ms. notes at R.I.

381   Experimental researches in electricity. 23rd series. 29. On the polar or other condition of diamagnetic bodies.

> *Phil. trans.* 1850: 171–88 (read March 7 and 14).
> *Phil. mag.* 1850, **37**: 88–108.
> *See also* no. 297.

382   On some points of domestic chemical philosophy—a fire, a candle, a lamp, a chimney, a kettle, ashes.

> A course of 6 lectures at R.I., April 27–June 1, cf. *B-J* **2**: 256–57.
> Ms. notes at R.I.
> *Yrbk. facts* 1851: 80, a report of the lecture, "On a chimney".

383   On certain conditions of freezing water; or, on the philosophy of water and ice.

> *Ath.* 1850: 640–41 (no. 1181, June 15).
> Abstract (by F.) of the lecture at R.I. on June 7.
> Reprinted in *Experimental researches in chemistry and physics.*
> Ms. notes at R.I.

384   Experimental researches in electricity. 24th–27th series. 30. On the possible relation of gravity to electricity. 31. On the magnetic and diamagnetic condition of bodies. 32. Magnetic conducting power. 33. Atmospheric magnetism.

> *Phil. trans.* 1851: 1–122 (read 1850, Nov. 28).
> *See also* no. 297.

385   Report of the Commission appointed to inquire into the state of the pictures in the National Gallery. (*In: Report of the Select Committee appointed to consider the present accommodation afforded by the National Gallery . . .* 1850. pp. 67–69. Appendix A.)

> *Parl. pap.* 1850 (612) xv.
> The Commission reported on May 24, 1850. F. was one of its three members.

5. FARADAY'S LABORATORY IN THE BASEMENT OF THE ROYAL INSTITUTION
Top: The Chemical Laboratory as it was in 1819. Off to the right through the large arch was a small lecture theatre
Bottom: Faraday's "Dark Room", leading off from the Chemical Laboratory, where he did his electrical and magnetic researches. (From a watercolour by Harriet Moore about 1850)

386 Report of the Select Committee appointed to consider the present accommodation afforded by the National Gallery and the best mode of preserving and exhibiting to the public works of art.

> *Parl. pap.* 1850 (612) xv.
> F's evidence pp. 44–48. He appeared before the Select Committee on July 4.

1851

387 On the magnetic characters and relations of oxygen and nitrogen.

> *R.I. proc.* 1851–54, **1**: 1–4.
> Abstract of lecture at R.I. on Jan. 24.
> Ms. notes at R.I.

388 On atmospheric magnetism.

> *R.I. proc.* 1851–54, **1**: 56–60.
> Signed M.F.
> Abstract of lecture at R.I. on April 11.
> Reprinted in *Experimental researches in electricity*, v. **3**.

389 Six lectures on some points of electrical philosophy, May 3–June 7, at Royal Institution.

> cf. *B-J* **2**: 280.
> Ms. notes at R.I.

390 Electric currents in plants.

> *R.I. proc.* 1851–54, **1**: 75–76.
> Report of lecture at R.I. on May 16.

391 Artificial production of the ruby, etc.

> *R.I. proc.* 1851–54, **1**: 83–84.
> Signed M.F.
> Abstract of lecture at R.I. on May 23.

392 On Schönbein's ozone.

> *R.I. proc.* 1851–54, **1**: 94–97.
> *Chem. gaz.* 1851, **9**: 258–60.
> Abstract (by F.) of lecture at R.I. on June 13.
> Ms. notes at R.I.

393 On a specimen of dark glass which was found to be melted after being placed outside the eye-piece of a telescope.

> *Brit. Assoc. rep.* 1851 (pt. 2): 22–23.
> Abstract of a report "submitted on the part of Dr. Roxburgh". The Association met from July 2–8.

394 Experimental researches in electricity. 28th series. 36. On lines of magnetic force; their definite character; and their distribution within a magnet and through space.

> *Phil. trans.* 1852: 25–56 (read 1851, Nov. 27 and Dec. 11).
>
> *See also* no. 297.
>
> *Note:* Section 36 is numbered Section 34 in the collected ed.

395 Syllabus of a course of six lectures on attractive forces, adapted to a juvenile auditory, . . . December 27, 1851–January 8 [1852]. Royal Institution of Great Britain, December, 1851.

> Handbill. 14×11 cm.
>
> Ms. notes at R.I.; their title indicates F. used same notes for Christmas lectures 1856–57. *See* no. 433.

395a Letter dated R.I. 28th Dec. 1835. (*In: Northern Lighthouses; returns of several applications made to the Commissioners of Northern Lights . . . pp. 66–67.*)

> *Parl. pap.* 1851 (18) lii.
>
> Signed W. Faraday. (*See* Introduction p. xx.)
>
> On the action of seawater on cast iron and bronze, and proposed materials for the construction of lighthouses.

1852

396 On the lines of magnetic force.

> *R.I. proc.* 1851–54, **1**: 105–8.
>
> Signed M.F.
>
> Abstract of lecture at R.I. on Jan. 23.
>
> Reprinted in *Experimental researches in electricity*, v. **3**.
>
> Ms. notes at R.I.

397 Remarks on a diaphragm steam generator, on boiler explosions, and on the process of combustion.

> *Min. proc. Instn. Civ. Engrs.* 1851–52, **11**: 398, 403.
>
> Abstract of discussion at a meeting of the Institution on March 23.

398 Experimental researches in electricity. 29th series. 35. On the employment of the induced magneto-electric current as a test and measure of magnetic forces.

> *Phil. trans.* 1852: 137–59 (read March 25 and April 1).
>
> *See also* no. 297.

399 The subject matter of a course of six lectures on the non-metallic elements. Delivered before the members of the Royal Institution, in the spring and summer of 1852. Arranged, by permission, from the lecturer's notes, lent for the occasion by J. Scoffern. To which is appended, remarks on the

quality and tendencies of chemical philosophy, on allotropism, and ozone; together with manipulative details relating to the performance of experiments indicated by Professor Faraday. London: Longman, Brown, Green, and Longmans, 1853.

> viii, 293 pp. illus. 18 cm.
> Binder's title, Faraday's lectures.
> These lectures were from April 24–June 5.
> Ms. notes at R.I.

400   On the physical lines of magnetic force.

> *R.I. proc.* 1851–54, **1**: 216–20.
> Signed M.F.
> A lecture at the R.I. on June 11.
> Reprinted in *Experimental researches in electricity*, v. **3**.
> Ms. notes at R.I.

401   On the physical character of the lines of magnetic force.

> *Phil. mag.* 1852, **3**: 401–28 (June).
> Reprinted in *Experimental researches in electricity*, v. **3**.

401a   Letter to the Secretary, Trinity House, dated R.I. 27 Sept., 1852, on Nash Low lighthouse struck by lightning.

> *Lightning Rod Conference (1878–1881)*. Edited by G. J. Symons. London, 1882, pp. 187–89.

402   A course of six lectures on chemistry, adapted to a juvenile auditory . . . December 28, 1852–January 8 [1853]. Royal Institution of Great Britain, December, 1852.

> Handbill. 13 × 10 cm.
> An account of the last of these lectures given in *Mech. mag.* 1853, **58**: 68–69 (no. 1537, Jan. 22).
> *Yrbk. facts* 1854: 144–45 (the same).
> Ms. notes at R.I.

1853

403   Observations on the magnetic force.

> *R.I. proc.* 1851–54, **1**: 229–38.
> Signed M.F.
> *Phil. mag.* 1853, **5**: 218–27.
> Abstract of lecture at R.I. on Jan. 21.
> Reprinted in *Experimental researches in electricity*, v. **3**, with omission of last three paragraphs.
> Ms. notes at R.I.

403a Eddystone Light; report on electrical phenomenon which occurred thereat
on 11 Jan., 1853.

> *Lightning Rod Conference (1878–1881)*. Edited by G. J. Symons. London, 1882, pp.
> 189–91.
> Letter to the Secretary, Trinity House, dated R.I. 24 Jan., 1853.

404 Remarks on the use of heated air as a motive power.

> *Min. proc. Instn. Civ. Engrs.* 1852–53, **12**: 348–49.
> Abstract of discussion at meetings of the Institution, Feb. 15–22.

405 Six lectures at R.I. on static electricity, April 9–May 14.

> *Morning chronicle*, 1853, April 11: 5 etc.
> Not seen; copy at BM Newspaper Library, Colindale.
> Ms. notes at R.I.

406 Mm. Boussingault, Frémy, Becquerel, etc., on oxygen.

> *R.I. proc.* 1851–54, **1**: 337–39.
> Signed M.F.
> Abstract of lecture at R.I. on June 10.
> Ms. notes at R.I.

407 On table turning.

> *The Times*, 1853, June 30: 8d.
> Letter dated R.I. June 28.
> Reprinted in *Experimental researches in chemistry and physics*.
> *See* note to no. 408.

408 Experimental investigation of table-turning.

> *Ath.* 1853: 801–03 (no. 1340, July 2).
> Dated R.I. June 27.
> Reprinted in *Experimental researches in chemistry and physics*.
> *Note:* Nos. 407 and 408 reprinted in *Scientific monthly*, 1956, **83**: 145–50, with title "Michael
> Faraday's researches in spiritualism".

409 Syllabus of a course of six lectures on voltaic electricity adapted to a
juvenile auditory . . . December 27th, 1853–January 5th [1854]. Royal
Institution of Great Britain, December, 1853.

> Handbill. 14·5×11 cm.
> Ms. notes at R.I.

410 Report of a Select Committee appointed to inquire into the management
of the National Gallery . . . 1853.

> *Parl. pap.* 1852–53 (867) xxxv.
> F's evidence pp. 373–83.

See 399 The subject matter of a course of six lectures on the non-metallic
elements. Delivered before members of the Royal Institution, in the spring
and summer of 1852. London, 1853.

411 On electric induction:—Associated cases of current and static effects.

> *R.I. proc.* 1851–54, **1**: 345–55.
> *Phil. mag.* 1854, **7**: 197–208.
> Lecture at R.I. on Jan. 20.
> Reprinted in *Experimental researches in electricity*, v. **3**.

412 Propriétés électriques remarquables des fils de cuivre recouverts de gutta percha. Extrait d'une lettre au professeur de la Rive.

> *Bibl. univ. Arch.* 1854, **25**: 169–70 (Feb.).
> Letter dated R.I. Jan. 28, and given in English in *B-J* **2**: 317-19.

413 An account of Schönbein's researches on the action of temperature on physical bodies.

> *R.I. proc.* 1851–54, **1**: 400.
> Account of a lecture at a general monthly meeting of the R.I. on March 6.

414 Sur le développement des courants induits dans les liquides. Lettre à M. de la Rive.

> *Bibl. univ. Arch.* 1854, **25**: 267–74 (March).
> *Ann. chim.* 1854, **41**: 196–98.
> Letter dated R.I. March 7, 1854.
> English translation with title, "On electro-dynamic induction in liquids", in *Phil. mag.* 1854, **7**: 265–68.
> Also in *B-J* **2**: 325-31.

415 Observations on mental education. (*In: Lectures on education delivered at the Royal Institution of Great Britain*. London, John W. Parker, 1854, pp. 39–88.)

> A lecture on May 6.
> Reprinted in *Experimental researches in chemistry and physics*.

1855
(A reprint of the 1854 ed.)

1867
Observations on the education of the judgement. A lecture delivered at the Royal Institution of Great Britain. By Professor Faraday. Originally published under the title of Observations on mental education. (*In: Modern culture; its true aims and requirements. A series of addresses and arguments on the claims of scientific education* . . . Ed. by Edward L. Youmans. London, Macmillan, 1867, pp. (192)–230.)

> An American ed. of Youmans was published in New York by D. Appleton, 1867, with title, *The culture demanded by modern life.* . . . F's lecture is pp. 187–224.

1917
Observations on mental education. . . . (*In: Science and education: lectures delivered at the Royal Institution of Great Britain*. Ed. with an introduction by Sir E. Ray Lankester. London, W. Heinemann (1917), pp. 39–67.)

416   On magnetic hypotheses.

> *R.I. proc.* 1851–54, **1**: 457–59.
> *Mech. mag.* 1854, **61**: 6–7.
> Abstract (by F.) of lecture at R.I. on June 9.
> Reprinted in *Experimental researches in electricity*, v. **3**.
> Ms. notes at R.I.

417   On subterraneous electro-telegraph wires.

> *Phil. mag.* 1854, **7**: 396–98 (June).
> Reprinted in *Experimental researches in electricity*, v. **3**.

418   On lightning conductors.

> *Brit. Assoc. rep.* 1854 (pt. 2): 158.
> Editorial note of comment by F. on Nasmyth's description of a lightning conductor for chimneys.
> B.A. meeting was Sept. 20–27.

419   Syllabus of a course of six lectures on the chemistry of combustion, adapted to a juvenile auditory . . . December 28th, 1854–January 9th [1855]. Royal Institution of Great Britain, December, 1854.

> Handbill. 14 × 11 cm.
> Ms. notes at R.I.
> F. used same notes for Christmas lectures of 1848–49 and 1860–61, *see* nos. 372 and 464.

1855

420   On some points of magnetic philosophy.

> *R.I. proc.* 1854–58, **2**: 6–13.
> Signed M.F.
> A lecture at R.I. on Jan. 22.
> Reprinted in *Experimental researches in electricity*, v. **3**.
> Ms. notes at R.I.

421   On some points of magnetic philosophy.

> *Phil. mag.* 1855, **9**: 81–113 (Feb.).
> Reprinted in *Experimental researches in electricity*, v. **3**.

422   Further observations on associated cases, in electric induction, of current and static effects.

> *Phil. mag.* 1855, **9**: 161–65 (March).
> Reprinted in *Experimental researches in electricity*, v. **3**.

423   Magnetic remarks.

> *Phil. mag.* 1855, **9**: 253–55 (April).

6. FARADAY'S STUDY ON THE SECOND FLOOR OF THE ROYAL INSTITUTION
Top: From the watercolour by Harriet Moore
Bottom: The same study as it is today, from the watercolour by Sir Lawrence Bragg

424 On electric conduction.

> *R.I. proc.* 1854–58, **2**: 123–32.
> Signed M.F.
> *Phil. mag.* 1855, **10**: 98–107.
> A lecture at R.I. on May 25.
> Ms. notes at R.I.

425 On Ruhmkorff's induction apparatus.

> *R.I. proc.* 1854–58, **2**: 139–42.
> Signed M.F.
> Abstract of lecture at R.I. on June 8.
> Ms. notes at R.I.

426 On the state of the Thames.

> *The Times*, 1855, July 9: 8f.
> *Mech. mag.* 1855, **63**: 28 (no. 1666, July 14).
> Letter dated R.I. July 7.
> Reprinted in *B-J* **2**: 358–59.

427 Experimental researches in electricity. 30th series. 38. Constancy of differential magnecrystallic force in different media. 39. Action of heat on magnecrystals. 40. Effect of heat upon the absolute magnetic force of bodies.

> *Phil. trans.* 1856: 159–80 (read 1855, Nov. 15 and 22).
> *Note:* Secs. 38–40 are not included in the collected ed. (no. 297). Sec. 36 is re-numbered Sec. 34 and two new paragraphs appear: Sec. 36, On the amount and general disposition of the forces of a magnet . . ., and Sec. 37, Delineation of lines of magnetic force by iron filings.
> R.I. has a 4 v. inter-leaved collection of offprints of *Experimental researches in electricity* and of other papers, with annotations by F.

428 Syllabus of a course of six lectures on the distinctive properties of the common metals, adapted to a juvenile auditory . . . 27th December, 1855–8th January [1856]. Royal Institution of Great Britain, December, 1855.

> Handbill. 13·5 × 10·5 cm.
> Ms. notes at R.I. The same notes were used for the Christmas lectures of 1858–59, *see* no. 450.

See 297 Experimental researches in electricity, v. 3. London, 1855.

See 415 Observations on mental education. (*In: Lectures on education delivered at the Royal Institution.* London, 1855.)

1856

429 On the action of non-conducting bodies in electric induction. By Professor Faraday and Dr. P. Reiss.

> *Phil. mag.* 1856, **11**: 1–17 (Jan.).
> Consists of letter from F. to Reiss, dated London, Nov. 19, 1855 and reply from Reiss, dated Berlin, Dec. 10, 1855. Footnotes by F.

430 On certain magnetic actions and affections.

> *R.I. proc.* 1854–58, **2**: 196–98.
> Signed M.F.
> *Pharm. j.* 1855–56, **15**: 476–77.
> *Phil. mag.* 1856, **11**: 322–24.
> Abstract of lecture at R.I. on Feb. 22.
> Ms. notes at R.I.

431 Letter to W. Wright about contribution to London Female Dormitory.

> *Notes and queries,* 4th series, 1873, **11**: 73.
> Dated R.I. 1856, March 11.

432 On M. Petitjean's process for silvering glass; some observations on divided gold.

> *R.I. proc.* 1854–58, **2**: 308–12.
> Signed M.F.
> Abstract of lecture at R.I. on June 13.
> Ms. notes at R.I.

433 Syllabus of a course of six lectures on attraction, adapted to a juvenile auditory . . . 27th December, 1856–8th January, 1857. Royal Institution of Great Britain, December, 1856.

> Handbill. 15 × 11·5 cm.
> Ms notes at R.I.: the same notes as for Christmas lectures 1851–52. *See* no. 395.

1857

434 Remarks on electric currents and induction in submarine telegraphs.

> *Min. proc. Instn. Civ. Engrs.* 1856–57, **16**: 220–22.
> Abstract of discussion at meeting of the Institution on Jan. 13.

435 Experimental relations of gold, and other metals, to light.

> *Phil. trans.* 1857: 145–81 (read Feb. 5).
> *Phil. mag.* 1857, **14**: 401–17, 512–39.
> Reprinted in *Experimental researches in chemistry and physics.*
> Reprinted in part in *The foundations of colloid chemistry; a selection of early papers.* . . . Ed. by Emil Hatschek. London, E. Benn, 1925, pp. 65–92. "Only that part of the paper dealing with dispersions of gold in aqueous medium is here reprinted."
> Ms. notes at R.I.

436 On the conservation of force.

> *R.I. proc.* 1854–58, **2**: 352–65.
> Signed M.F.
> *Phil. mag.* 1857, **13**: 225–39.
> A lecture at R.I. on Feb. 27.
> Reprinted in *Experimental researches in chemistry and physics,* with an additional note, pp. 460–63. This note also appears in *Phil. mag.* 1859, **17**: 166–69 (*see* no. 452).

1865

Some thoughts on the conservation of force. (*In: The correlation and conservation of forces: a series of expositions, by Prof. Grove, Prof. Helmholtz, Dr. Mayer, Dr. Faraday, Prof. Liebig and Dr. Carpenter. With an introduction and brief biographical notices of the chief promoters of the new views. By Edward L. Youmans. New York, D. Appleton, 1865, pp. 357–83.*)

437 On a ready method of determining the presence, position, depth, and length of a needle broken into the foot. Communicated by H. Bence-Jones.

> *Proc. R. Med. Chir. Soc.* 1856–57, **1**: 71–74 (1857, March 10).
> The method, using a magnetized test needle, is explained in a letter from "a scientific friend". That this was F. is indicated in *B-J* **2**: 388.

438 Brief account of Mr. C. V. Walker's electric telegraph for railways.

> *R.I. proc.* 1854–58, **2**: 403.
> Signed M.F.
> Lecture at R.I. on March 20.

See 445 Letter to Dean of St. Paul's, on the state of the marbles in the British Museum. Dated R.I. April 30.

439 A course of six lectures on static electricity.

> Lectures at R.I. after Easter, see *B-J* **2**: 388.
> Easter Sunday was April 12.

See 476 Reports on electric light by order of Trinity House, April–May, 1857.

440 Twinkling of the stars.

> *Phil. mag.* 1857, **13**: 301 (April).
> Signed M.F.

441 On the relations of gold to light.

> *R.I. proc.* 1854–58, **2**: 444–46.
> Signed M.F.
> Abstract of lecture at R.I. on June 12.
> Ms. notes at R.I.
> cf. no. 435.

442 On the persistent appearance of the lightning flash.

> *Phil. mag.* 1857, **13**: 506 (June).
> Signed M.F.

443 Note on the irregular fusibility of ice. (*In: On some physical properties of ice. By John Tyndall.*)

> *Phil. trans.* 1858: 228–29 (read 1857, Dec. 17).
> *Phil. mag.* 1858, **16**: 354–56.
> Reprinted in *Experimental researches in chemistry and physics.*

444 Syllabus of a course of lectures on static electricity, adapted to a juvenile auditory . . . 29th December, 1857–9th January [1858]. Royal Institution of Great Britain, December, 1857.

> Handbill. 14·5 × 11·5 cm.
> Ms. notes at R.I.

445 Report of the National Gallery site commission, together with the minutes, evidence, appendix and index. Presented to both Houses of Parliament by Command.

> *Parl. pap.* 1857, session 2[2261] xxiv.
> F. was a member of this Commission.
> P. (149) a letter from F. to the Dean of St. Paul's, on the state of the marbles in the British Museum, dated R.I., April 30, 1857.

1858

446 Remarks on static induction.

> *R.I. proc.* 1854–58, **2**: 470–75, 490–91.
> Signed M.F.
> Abstract of lecture at R.I. on Feb. 12, with additional note, dated March 22, pp. 490–91.
> Ms. notes at R.I.

447 On Wheatstone's Electric Telegraph in relation to science, being an argument in favour of the full recognition of science as a branch of education.

> *R.I. proc.* 1854–58, **2**: 555–60.
> Lecture at R.I. on June 11.
> Ms. notes at R.I.

448 University of London. Report of the Committee appointed to consider the propriety of establishing a degree or degrees in science, and the conditions on which such degree or degrees should be conferred, with the evidence taken before the Committee. n.p., n.d.

> viii (138) pp. 21 cm.
> Separate from (printed) Minutes of the Senate?
> The Committee was appointed by the Senate on April 14, 1858 and reported in July. Its members were: the Chancellor, the Vice Chancellor, Dr. Arnott, Mr. Brande, Sir James Clark, Mr. Faraday, Mr. Grote and Mr. Walker.

449 On the glaciers of Switzerland.

> *The Times*, 1858, Sept. 3: 10e.
> Letter dated R.I. Sept. 2. Signed W. Faraday, but *B-J* **2**: 402–3 shows this a misprint for Michael F. (*see* Introduction p. xx).

450 Syllabus of a course of six lectures, adapted to a juvenile auditory, on metalline properties; illustrated by such metals as in virtue of these properties are applied to useful and important services . . . 28th December, 1858–8th January [1859]. Royal Institution of Great Britain, December, 1858.

> Handbill. 19·5 × 12 cm.
> *See B-J* **2**: 417 for F's reasons for refusing to publish these lectures (*see* Introduction pp. xvii–xviii). Ms. notes at R.I. F. used the same notes for the Christmas lectures of 1855-56, *see* no. 428.

1859

451 On Schönbein's ozone and antozone.

> *R.I. proc.* 1858–62, **3**: 70–71.
> Signed M.F.
> Abstract of lecture at R.I. on Feb. 25.

452 On regelation, and on the conservation of force.

> *Phil. mag.* 1859, **17**: 162–69 (March).
> "The volume of reprinted *Experimental researches in chemistry and physics*, by Prof. Faraday which has just been published, contains the following new matter. . . ." (Introductory editorial note.)
> *See also* no. 436.

See 474 and 476 Report on the magneto-electric light established by Professor Holmes at the High lighthouse, South Foreland. Dated R.I. April 29.

453 Six lectures on the various forces of matter.

> A course of lectures at the R.I. after Easter (Easter Day April 24). cf. *B-J* **2**: 417.
> *See also* no. 457.

454 On phosphorescence, fluorescence, etc.

> *R.I. proc.* 1858–62, **3**: 159–63.
> Signed M.F.
> *Photog. Soc. j.* 1860, **6**: 42–45.
> Abstract of lecture at R.I. on June 17.
> Ms. notes at R.I.

See 466 Letter to Mr. Bonham Carter of 8th July 1859 relating to the process for preserving the stone in the New Palace at Westminster.

455 Report of the proceedings of the Balloon committee of the British Association appointed at the meeting at Leeds.

> *Brit. Assoc. rep.* 1859 (pt. 1): 289–91.
> Report of a meeting on May 27. F. a member of this Committee. B.A. meeting held Sept. 14-21, 1859.

456 On water in lighthouses.

> *The Times*, 1859, Sept. 24: 9d.
> *J. Soc. Arts*, 1858–59, **7**: 707–8.
> Letter dated R.I. Sept. 22.

See 465   Account of a mode of purifying water contaminated by lead, contained in a letter to the Inspector General of Fortifications.

> Dated R.I. 1859, Oct. 7.

457   A course of six lectures adapted to a juvenile auditory, consisting of illustrations of the various forces of matter, i.e. of such as are called the physical or inorganic forces—including an account of their relations to each other. Reported verbatim by special permission.

> *Chem. news* 1860, **1**: 52–55, 65–68, 77–80, 88–91, 100–3, 126–29.
>
> Christmas lectures at R.I. Dec. 27, 1859–Jan. 7, 1860.
>
> Ms. notes at R.I.

1860

A course of six lectures on the various forces of matter and their relations to each other. Delivered before a juvenile auditory at the Royal Institution of Great Britain during the Christmas Holidays of 1859–60. Ed. by William Crookes. With numerous illustrations. London, Glasgow, Richard Griffin, 1860.

> (viii) 179 pp. illus. 17 cm.
>
> Lecture on lighthouse illumination, delivered before the R.I. 1860, March 9, pp. 155–74 (*see* no. 460).
>
> A reprint of the lectures from *Chem. news.*
>
> "[The lectures] are printed as they were spoken, *verbatim et literatim*. A careful and skilful reporter took them down, and the manuscript, as deciphered from his notes, was subsequently most carefully corrected by the Editor. . . ." (Editor's preface, p. v.)

1860

2nd ed.

1861

3rd ed.

> *Note: The English catalogue of books* gives date of 3rd ed. as 1862.

1863

Lectures on the various forces of matter and on the chemical history of a candle. Delivered before a juvenile auditory at the Royal Institution of Great Britain during the Christmas Holidays of 1859–60–61. London, Griffin, Bohn, 1863.

> (viii) 179 (iii)–viii, 208 pp. plates, illus. 17 cm.
>
> Binder's title: Faraday before a juvenile audience.
>
> Includes Lecture on lighthouse illumination (no. 460) pp. 155–74 (first series), and Lecture on platinum (no. 468), pp. 173–204 (second series).
>
> *See* no. 464 for lectures on chemical history of a candle.
>
> *Note:* A later ed. of Lectures on the various forces of matter was published by Chatto and Windus in 1874, with reprints in 1876, 1881 and 1894 (information from Chatto and Windus) under the title, *On the various forces of nature.* All lack indication of their date of publication. The two copies described below appear to be variant issues of the 1874 ed. This assumption is based on the difference in imprint together with the accession date of the BM copy. *See also* Introduction, p. xiii.

1874 (1st issue?)
On the various forces of nature and their relations to each other: a course of lectures delivered before a juvenile audience at the Royal Institution. Ed. by William Crookes. With numerous illustrations. London: Chatto and Windus, successors to John Camden Hotten, n.d.

> 200 pp. illus. 17·5 cm. (but copy rebound).
> Includes Lecture on lighthouse illumination (no. 460), pp. (173)–93.

1874 (2nd issue?)
On the various forces of nature. . . . Ed. by William Crookes. A new edition, with illustrations. London: Chatto and Windus, Piccadilly, n.d.

> 200 pp. illus. 18·5 cm.
> Includes Lecture on lighthouse illumination (no. 460), pp. (173)–93.
> The British Museum's copy, where accessioned on Jan. 7, 1874.

1876
1881 } see *Note* above.
1894

458 Experimental researches in chemistry and physics. Reprinted from the *Philosophical transactions* of 1821–1857; the *Journal of the Royal Institution*; the *Philosophical magazine*, and other publications. London, Richard Taylor and William Francis, Red Lion Court, Fleet Street, 1859.

> vii, 496 pp. illus. plates. 23 cm.
> F's own copy, with his ms. notes, including notes of other articles by him not here included, is in the library of the Institution of Electrical Engineers.

459 Report of a Commission appointed to consider the subject of lighting picture galleries with gas.

> *Parl. pap.* 1859, session 2 (106) xv.
> A William Faraday is indicated as being a member of this Commission. This is evidently a misprint for Michael, for *B-J* 2: 418 says that F. was a member. (*See* Introduction p. xx.) *See also* no. 471.

1860

See 476 Reports on South Foreland electric light, 1860, Feb.–1861, Jan.

460 On lighthouse illumination—the electric light.

> *Chem. news* 1860, **1**: 171–74.
> Lecture at R.I. on March 9.
> Reprinted in eds. of *A course of six lectures on the various forces of matter* from 1860 onwards. *See* no. 457.
> Abstract in *R.I. proc.* 1858–62, **3**: 220–23; *Phil. mag.* 1860, **19**: 320–23.
> Ms. notes at R.I.

461 Note on a possible relation of gravity with electricity or heat.

> Dated April 16, 1860. Received by Royal Society on June 7, but not published. See *B-J* **2**: 411–12.
>
> Ms. not seen.

462 Note on regelation.

> *Roy. Soc. proc.* 1859–60, **10**: 440–50 (read April 26).
> *Phil. mag.* 1861, **21**: 146–53.

463 On the electric silk-loom.

> *R.I. proc.* 1858–62, **3**: 271–74.
> Signed M.F.
> *Chem. news* 1860, **2**: 235–36.
> Abstract of lecture at R.I. on June 8.
> Ms. notes at R.I.

464 A course of six lectures, adapted to a juvenile auditory, on the chemical history of a candle. Reported verbatim by special permission.

> *Chem. news* 1861, **3**: 6–10, 24–27, 42–46, 57–60, 72–76, 84–88.
> Christmas lectures at R.I. Dec. 27, 1860–Jan. 8, 1861.
> Ms. notes at R.I. F. used same notes for Christmas lectures of 1848–49 and 1854–55, *see* nos. 372 and 419.

1861

A course of six lectures on the chemical history of a candle: to which is added a lecture on platinum. Delivered before a juvenile auditory at the Royal Institution of Great Britain during the Christmas holidays of 1860–1. Ed. by William Crookes. With numerous illustrations. London, Griffin, Bohn, 1861.

> viii, 208 pp. illus. 17·5 cm.
> Lecture on platinum, delivered at R.I. 1861, Feb. 22, pp. 173–204 (*see* no. 468). A reprint of the lectures from *Chem. news*.

1862

(Another ed.)

> Listed in *English catalogue of books*. Not seen.

1863

See 457 Lectures on the various forces of matter and on the chemical history of a candle. . . . London, Griffin, Bohn, 1863.

1865

A course of six lectures on the chemical history of a candle: to which is added a lecture on platinum. Delivered . . . 1860–1. Ed. by William Crookes. With numerous illustrations. London, Charles Griffin, 1865.

> viii, 208 pp. illus. 17·5 cm.
> Lecture on platinum (no. 468), pp. 173–204.

1874–1896

The chemical history of a candle: a course of lectures delivered before a juvenile audience at the Royal Institution. Ed. by William Crookes. A new ed. with illustrations. London, Chatto and Windus, Piccadilly, n.d.

> x (13)–226 pp. illus. 18·5 cm.
>
> Includes Lecture on platinum (no. 468), pp. 191–222.
>
> Date of publication confirmed by Chatto and Windus. This 1874 ed. was subsequently reprinted by Chatto and Windus in 1876, 1880, 1894 and 1896. *See* Introduction, p. xxiii.

1904

The chemical history of a candle. . . . London, Unit Library, 1904.

> 117 pp. illus. 16·5 cm. (The Unit Library, no. 37.)
>
> Lecture on platinum not included.

1907

The chemical history of a candle. . . . London, Hutchinson, 1907.

> 117 pp. front. illus. 17·5 cm. (Hutchinson's Popular Classics.)
>
> Text pages identical with those of 1904 ed.

1908

The chemical history of a candle: a course of lectures delivered before a juvenile audience at the Royal Institution. Ed. by William Crookes. A new impression, with illus. London, Chatto and Windus, 1908.

> x, 14–226 pp. illus. 18 cm.
>
> Includes Lecture on platinum (no. 468), pp. 191–222.

1920

The chemical history of a candle. Ed. by W. R. Fielding. . . . London, J. M. Dent [1920].

> (ii) 158 pp. front. illus. 15·5 cm. (The Kings Treasuries of Literature.)
>
> "For this ed. I have rearranged Sir William Crookes' transcription of Faraday's Lectures . . . and have provided it with a few necessary connecting links. The result has been divided into sections, and new figures have been added. . . ." (Editor's note.) Date is that of *British Museum Catalogue* and *English catalogue of books*. Lecture on platinum not included.

1933

The chemical history of a candle. Put into Basic English by Phyllis Rossiter. London, Kegan Paul, Trench, Trubner, 1933.

> 152 (1) pp. diagrs. 15·5 cm. (Psyche Miniatures. General series, no. 61.)
>
> ". . . the first complete book on science to be put into the limits of the 850 word list . . . [in addition] a special list of 100 names for General Science and 50 for the special field of Physics and Chemistry has been used." (To the reader, p. 7.)

*465 Account of a mode of purifying water contaminated by lead, contained in a letter to the Inspector General of Fortifications.

> *Papers on subjects connected with the duties of the Corps of Royal Engineers* . . . 1860, new series **9**: 47–48.
>
> *Yrbk. facts*, 1861: 177–78.
>
> Dated R.I. 1859, Oct. 7.

See 457 A course of six lectures on the various forces of matter. . . . London, Glasgow, Richard Griffin, 1860.

A course of six lectures on the various forces of matter. . . . 2nd ed . . . 1860.

466 Letter to Mr. Bonham Carter of 8 July 1859, relating to the process for preserving the stone in the New Palace at Westminster.

> *Parl. pap.* 1860 (475) xl.

467 Report of Sir Roderick Murchison and Professor Faraday on the processes for preserving external stonework of Houses of Parliament. . . .

> *Parl. pap.* 1860 (309) xl.

On the preservation of stone.

> *The Times,* 1860, Dec. 25: 8f.
> A reprint of letter to Frederick Ransome dated R.I. Dec. 6 (in Report).

1861

468 On platinum.

> *Chem. news* 1861, **3**: 136–41.
> Lecture at R.I. on Feb. 22.
> Reprinted in some eds. of *The chemical history of a candle (see* no. 464).
> Abstract in *R.I. proc.* 1858–62, **3**: 321–22.
> Ms. notes at R.I.

469 On the solar eclipse of July 18, 1860.

> *Chem. news* 1861, **3**: 334–38.
> Lecture at R.I. on May 3.
> *Note:* Abstract (by Faraday) of this lecture in *R.I. proc.* 1858–62, **3**: 362–66, has title: "On Mr Warren de la Rue's photographic eclipse results".
> Ms. notes at R.I.

470 Letter to Sir Emerson Tennent on spiritualism. (*In: Letter on Faraday and the spiritualists.* By John Tyndall.)

> *Pall Mall gaz.* 1868, **7**: 1750 (no. 1012, May 9).
> Dated Folkestone, 1861, June 14.

See 478 Report on Prosser's Lime Light at the South Foreland upper light.

> Dated R.I. 1861, Sept. 30.

471 Communications to the Lords of the Committee of Privy Council for Education by Professors Faraday, Tyndall, and Hoffman, with respect to lighting picture galleries with gas.

> *Parl. pap.* House of Lords 1861 (195) v.
> F. had been asked to re-observe the Sheepshanks Gallery. *See* no. 459. Signed William Faraday, *see* Introduction, p. xx.

See 464 A course of six lectures on the chemical history of a candle. . . . London, Griffin, Bohn, 1861.

See 457 A course of six lectures on the various forces of matter . . . 3rd ed. London, Glasgow, Richard Griffin, 1861.

472 Report of the Commissioners appointed to inquire into the condition and management of lights, buoys and beacons . . . 1861.

> *Parl. pap.* 1861 [2793] xxv.
> F's evidence v. **2**. Appendix, pp. 591–93.

473 Report, etc., to the Deputy-Master and Brethren of the Trinity House. (*In: Report of the Commissioners appointed to inquire into the condition and management of lights, buoys and beacons . . . 1861. Vol. 1, pp. 90–96.*)

> *Parl. pap.* 1861 [2793] xxv.
> *Contents:* Report on focal points; Report on experiments at Messrs. Chance's works [at Birmingham] and at Whitby, in relation to focal points; Report on experiments at Whitby in relation to the focal points of lighthouse apparatus; Report on the South lighthouse at Whitby; Report of experiments at Birmingham on the focal points of the lenticular panel of a fixed first order lighthouse apparatus; Report on the Smalls apparatus.

474 Report on the magneto-electric light established by Professor Holmes at the High lighthouse, South Foreland. (*In: Report of the Commissioners appointed to inquire into the condition and management of lights, buoys and beacons . . . 1861, pp. 2–4.*)

> *Parl. pap.* 1861 [2793] xxv.
> Also as Report no. 3 in Reports on the electric light, *Parl. pap.* 1862 (489) liv.

1862

See 476 Reports on the magneto-electric light at the Dungeness lighthouse.

> Dated R.I. Feb. 21, May 19 and July 5.

475 On gas-furnaces, etc.

> *R.I. proc.* 1858–62, **3**: 536–39.
> Signed M.F.
> *Chem. news* 1862, **6**: 53–55.
> *Phil. mag.* 1862, **24**: 162–65.
> Abstract (by F.) of lecture at R.I. on June 20.
> Ms. notes at R.I.

See 481 Evidence before the Commission appointed to inquire into the revenues and management of certain colleges and schools.

> F. gave evidence on Nov. 18.

See 464 A course of six lectures on the chemical history of a candle. . . . London, Griffin, Bohn, 1862.

> Not seen, but listed in *English catalogue of books*.

See *457*   A course of six lectures on the various forces of matter . . . 3rd ed. 1862.

> Not seen, but listed in *English catalogue of books.*

476   Reports on the electric light to the Royal Commissioners, and made by order of the Trinity Board.

> *Parl. pap.* 1862 (489) liv.
>
> *Contents:* Reports made by order of the Trinity Board, April–May, 1857 (nos. 1–2): Report on the magneto-electric light, established by Professor Holmes at the High lighthouse, South Foreland, April 29, 1859 (no. 3)=no. 474; South Foreland electric light, Feb. 1860–Jan. 1861 (reports nos. 4–8); Report on the magneto-electric light at the Dungeness lighthouse, Feb. 21, May 19 and July 5, 1862 (nos. 9–11).

1863

477   Letter to the Prince of Wales, dated R.I. Jan. 5.

> *R.I. proc.* 1862–66, **4**: 3.
>
> Reprinted in *B-J* **2**: 456–57.
>
> Letter invites the Prince to become an Honorary Member and Vice Patron of the R.I.

See *457*   Lectures on the various forces of matter and on the chemical history of a candle. . . . London, Griffin, Bohn, 1863.

478   Reports made to the Trinity House, by Professor Faraday and other persons in the service of that Corporation, relative to the Lime Light of the Universal Lime Light Company, exhibited at the South Foreland High lighthouse.

> *Parl. pap.* 1863 (344) lxiii.
>
> *Contents:* Report on Prosser's Lime Light at the South Foreland upper light, 1861 Sept. 30, and two other reports without titles.

479   Reports to the Trinity House upon the electric light now in operation at Dungeness. . . .

> *Parl. pap.* 1863 (216) lxiii.

1864

480   Mr. Faraday and spiritualism.

> *The Times,* 1864, Nov. 8: 9f.
>
> Letter dated R.I. Oct. 8.

481   Report of H.M. Commissioners appointed to inquire into the revenues and management of certain colleges and schools and the studies pursued and instruction given therein; with appendix and evidence.

> *Parl. pap.* 1864 [3288] xxi.
>
> F's evidence, given on Nov. 18, 1862, v. **4**, pt. 2, pp. 375–82.
>
> Extracts from F's evidence are reprinted in *Modern culture; its true aims and requirements.* Ed. by Edward L. Youmans. London, Macmillan, 1867, pp. 412–15. An American ed. of Youmans was published in New York by Appleton in 1867, with the title, *The culture demanded by modern life.*

7. A PHOTOGRAPH OF FARADAY IN 1863 AT THE AGE OF 72

See 464   A course of six lectures on the chemical history of a candle. . . . London, Charles Griffin, 1865.

See 436   Some thoughts on the conservation of force. (*In: The correlation and conservation of forces*. . . . New York, D. Appleton, 1865, pp. 357–83.)

1866

482   On the magneto-electric machine of the Alliance Company. (*In: Correspondence between the Board of Trade, the Lighthouse Boards, and other bodies or persons, concerning the electric light* . . . pp. 7–8.)

   Parl. pap. 1866 (313) lxvi.

1867

Note: F. died Aug. 25.

See 415   Observations on the education of the judgement. . . . (*In: Modern culture*. . . . Ed. by Edward L. Youmans. London, Macmillan, 1867, pp. (192)–230.)

   Note: American ed. published in New York by D. Appleton, 1867, with title, *The culture demanded by modern life*.

1874

See 464   The chemical history of a candle. . . . A new ed., with illustrations. London, Chatto and Windus, Piccadilly, n.d.

See 457   On the various forces of nature. . . . A new ed. London, Chatto and Windus, Piccadilly, n.d.

1876

See 464   The chemical history of a candle. . . . London, Chatto and Windus.

See 457   On the various forces of nature. . . . London, Chatto and Windus.

1878–1882?

See 297   Experimental researches in electricity. . . . 3 v. London, Bernard Quaritch, 1839–55. Facsimile reprint, n.d.

1880

See 464   The chemical history of a candle. . . . London, Chatto and Windus.

1881

See 457   On the various forces of nature. . . . London, Chatto and Windus.

1894

See 464 The chemical history of a candle. . . . London, Chatto and Windus.

See 457 On the various forces of nature. . . . London, Chatto and Windus.

1896

See 464 The chemical history of a candle. . . . London, Chatto and Windus.

483 The liquefaction of gases. Papers by Michael Faraday, 1823–1845. With an appendix consisting of papers by Thomas Northmore on the compression of gases, 1805–1806. Edinburgh, William F. Clay; London, Simpkin, Marshall, Hamilton, Kent, 1896.

> 79 pp. illus. 19 cm. (Alembic club reprint, no. 12.)
> A collected reprint of nos. 98, 99, 107 and 328.

1899

484 The fundamental laws of electrolytic conduction; memoirs by Faraday, Hittorf and F. Kohlrausch. Translated and ed. by H. M. Goodwin. New York and London, Harper and brothers, 1899.

> (8) (98) pp. diagrs. 21 cm. (*Harper's scientific memoirs*, ed. by J. S. Ames, no. 7).
> *Includes:* Relation by measure of common and voltaic electricity (*Experimental researches in electricity*, series 3. para. 8. No. 207), pp. 3–8. On electrochemical decomposition (*Experimental researches in electricity*, series 7. para. 11. No. 221), pp. 11–44; Biographical sketch, pp. 44–46.

485 The letters of Faraday and Schoenbein, 1836–1862. With notes, comments and references to contemporary letters. Ed. by Georg W. A. Kahlbaum and Francis V. Darbishire. Bâle, Benno Schwabe; London, Williams and Norgate, 1899.

> xvi, 376 (4) pp. front. (ports.) 23 cm.
> Reviewed in *Nature*, 1899–1900, **61**: 337.
> Includes all the letters to Schoenbein reprinted in Bence-Jones in addition to others.

1900

486 The discovery of induced electric currents, v. 2. Memoirs by Michael Faraday. Ed. by J. S. Ames. New York [etc.], American Book Co. (ᶜ1900).

> (vi) 96 pp. diagrs. 21 cm. (*Scientific memoirs*, ed. by J. S. Ames, no. 12.)
> *Includes:* "Faraday's discovery of induced currents" (reprint of *B-J* **2**: 1–6); *Experimental researches in electricity*, series 1. paras. 1–4 (no. 187); series 2. paras. 5–6 (no. 191); series 9. para. 15 (no. 234); series 14. para. 21 (no. 285); Biographical sketch, pp. 93–94.

1904

See 464 The chemical history of a candle. . . . London, Unit Library, 1904.

1907

See 464 The chemical history of a candle. . . . London, Hutchinson, 1907.

1908

See 464 The chemical history of a candle. . . . A new impression, with illus. London, Chatto and Windus, 1908.

1910

487 Select exhortations delivered to various Churches of Christ by the late Michael Faraday, Wm. Buchanan, John M. Baxter, and Alex. Moir. Dundee, John Leng, 1910.

> 138 pp. 18·5 cm.
>
> Edited by Dr. James Rorie of Dundee.
>
> Contains, pp. 15–37, "fragmentary notes" of 4 discourses delivered by F. In London: 1861, July 7 on Matt. xix, 16 and John xvii, 3; 1852, June 29 on Hebrews iii, 12 and 13; 1863, June 7 on Mark viii, 34. In Dundee: 1863, Aug. on John xi, 25 and 26.
>
> *See* Introduction, p. xix.

1912

See 297 Experimental researches in electricity. London, J. M. Dent, n.d. (Everyman's library.)

1917

See 415 Observations on mental education. (*In: Science and education.* . . . Ed. Sir E. Ray Lankester. London, W. Heinemann (1917), pp. 39–67.)

1920

See 464 The chemical history of a candle. Ed. by W. R. Fielding. . . . London, J. M. Dent, n.d. (The Kings Treasuries of Literature.)

1922

See 297 Experimental researches in electricity. London, J. M. Dent. (Everyman's library.)

> A reprint of the 1912 ed.

1925

See 435 On the experimental relations of gold to light. (*In: The foundations of colloid chemistry.* . . . Ed. by Emil Hatschek. London, E. Benn, 1925, pp. 65–92.)

See 297 Experimental researches in electricity. London, J. M. Dent. (Everyman's
Library.)

> A reprint of the 1912 ed.

488 A reproduction of some portions of Faraday's diary presented by the
Managers of the Royal Institution of Great Britain to [   ]
as a token of their appreciation of his presence at the Faraday celebrations
September 1931. [London, Royal Institution, 1931.]

> (24 pp.) illus. plates. 27 cm.

1932

489 Faraday's diary: being the various philosophical notes of experimental
investigation made by Michael Faraday during the years 1820–1862 and
bequeathed by him to the Royal Institution of Great Britain, now, by
order of the Managers, printed and published for the first time, under the
editorial supervision of Thomas Martin, with a foreword by Sir William
H. Bragg. London, G. Bell, 1932–36.

> 7 v.+Index. illus. plates. 26 cm.
>
> Reviewed in *Nature* by Allan Ferguson, 1932, **130**: 828–30; 1934, **133**: 627–28; 1935, **135**: 524–25; 1935, **136**: 739; 1936, **137**: 295–96.

1933

See 464 The chemical history of a candle. Put into Basic English by Phyllis
Rossiter. London, Kegan Paul [etc.], 1933. (Psyche Miniatures.)

1938–1951

See 297 Experimental researches in electricity. London, J. M. Dent. (Everyman's
library.)

> Reprints of the 1912 ed. were published in 1938, 1940, 1943 and 1951.

1956

See 407 and 408 Michael Faraday's researches in spiritualism.

> *Scientific monthly*, 1956, **83**: 145–50.
>
> A reprint of two articles from *The Times* and the *Athenaeum*, with an introduction.

INDEX

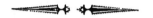

INDEX

NOTE: (1) This is *not* a subject index but a catchword title index to items in the bibliography. (2) *Arabic numbers* refer to *items* in the Bibliography, *Roman numbers* to *pages* of the Author's Introduction.

CPSIA information can be obtained
at www.ICGtesting.com
Printed in the USA
LVHW051519170120
644013LV00006BA/214